Contents

Introduction   2

Matthew 19–23   8
Dancing in the dark

Numbers 3–12   30
Pilgrims on the way

Numbers 13–19   44
So close, yet so far

Revelation 1–3   54
The Jesus letters

Revelation 4–11   67
The painful road to glory

Job 22–31   77
Finding hope in suffering

Job 32–42   92
The winner takes it all

Matthew 24,25   108
Waiting for his coming

SU article   4
Nurturing young faith

Spotlight on...   90
The wisdom books

Travelling together

Travel has been hit hard during the COVID-19 pandemic. At various times, British people have been told to stay at home. In France, people have had to carry a signed form explaining why they are away from home, and many other countries have had restrictions. So, it's appropriate that in this issue we'll do some travelling! Nigel Hopper takes us on a journey into Matthew's Gospel, part of what he calls Jesus' campaign trail. As we meet people along the way, we'll learn how Jesus responded to their queries and challenges.

A much earlier journey, in the book of Numbers, is explored by Richard Trist and Ben Green. As we travel with God's people towards the Promised Land, we'll be challenged to examine our own journey of faith. How much have we really learnt from God's past faithfulness? Tony Horsfall and David Lawrence then lead us through Revelation, the fascinating – and often mystifying – final book in the Bible. More than ever today, we need its powerful message, that God is in control and King Jesus reigns!

Jennie Pollock and John Gay guide us through the challenging book of Job. It addresses the fundamental question of why God allows suffering. Reading the book, we eavesdrop on a discussion between friends. Right at the end, God enters the debate and they are silenced. It's a warning not to jump to hasty conclusions. And strangely, that's useful advice for our last series. Alison Allen takes us to two chapters of Matthew, asking whether we're ready for Jesus' next coming.

We pray that your journey through this *Daily Bread* will be helpful and fruitful. As you travel, why not pray for the many thousands of other readers on this journey?

'Tricia and Emlyn Williams
Editors

Daily Bread toolbox

ricia & Emlyn
illiams
orked with
cripture Union
r many years.
nlyn led Schools
inistry, then
orked with SU
ternational.
icia was also
rt of the
hools team
d later worked
SU Publishing,
veloping,
iting and
iting Bible
sources.
ving recently
mpleted
earch in the
ea of faith
d dementia,
e continues
h writing and
ting faith
ources. Retired
m his role
discipleship
stor in a local
rch, Emlyn
v continues
writing and
king-with-
ple ministries.

WAY IN

This page introduces both the notes and the writer. It sets the scene and tells you what you need to know to get into each series.

A DAY'S NOTE

The notes for each day include five key elements: *Prepare, Read* (the Bible passage for the day), *Explore, Respond* and *Bible in a year*. These are intended to provide a helpful way of meeting God in his Word.

PREPARE

Prepare yourself to meet with God and pray that the Holy Spirit will help you to understand and respond to what you read.

READ

Read the Bible passage, taking time to absorb and simply enjoy it. A verse or two from the Bible text is usually included on each page, but it's important to read the whole passage.

EXPLORE

Explore the meaning of the passage, listening for what God may be saying to you. Before you read the comment, ask yourself: what is the main point of this passage? What is God showing me about himself or about my life? Is there a promise or a command, a warning or example to take special notice of?

RESPOND

Respond to what God has shown you in the passage in worship and pray for yourself and others. Decide how to share your discoveries with others.

BIBLE IN A YEAR

If your aim is to know God and his Word more deeply, why not follow this plan and read the whole Bible in one year?

Nurturing young faith

Children and young people who aren't in church need support, not just to explore faith but to respond and grow, too. Faith Guides and Grow Communities play a vital role in this process. SU Mission Enabler Neil Jackson, himself a Faith Guide, tells us more.

In the parable of the sower, Jesus explains that many things can threaten the development of a spiritual seed into a mature plant of faith. In the same way, if we introduce children and young people to Jesus but don't nurture and encourage them on their spiritual journey, they may falter before faith has the opportunity to develop.

That's what happened with Francesca – her family don't go to church, but she knew a bit about Jesus and Christian faith because she went to a Church of England primary school. Every Wednesday, a teacher would read a Bible story to the class and Francesca really enjoyed it. But when she moved on to secondary school, that Christian input ceased and so did her spiritual development.

Then she happened to meet my daughter Millie, who had just joined the same school. The two of them had lots of shared interests – art, drama, film – and quickly became firm friends. At Millie's invitation, Francesca started coming to Recharge, a monthly youth club I'd set up as a volunteer and Faith Guide with my church. It's aimed at young people without church backgrounds, so there are lots of activities for them to enjoy and a light touch of spiritual content.

Millie planned to go on SU's Quantum holiday the following summer, and asked Francesca if she'd like to accompany her. Francesca was keen, so off the two of them went for a few days of fun and faith exploration.

Faith is an unknown quantity, and so they are really open to investigating it.

A few years ago, young people often had negative perceptions of Christianity, but that's all changed now. Faith is an unknown quantity, and so they are really open to investigating it. That was certainly the case with Francesca; at Quantum she had a real curiosity to learn more, enjoyed Bible study time and didn't hesitate to ask the holiday leaders and Millie lots of questions! When they returned home, Francesca and Millie started reading and discussing the Bible together every week.

Grow Communities – a place for faith to develop and mature
Francesca continued coming to Recharge. A few months later, we added an extra session, Precharge, which Francesca joined. In the language of SU's new mission framework, Precharge is what we call a Grow Community. It's run and shaped by the young people themselves. Guided by adults, they explore and grow in faith in a setting and manner that works for them, rather than us expecting them to adapt to the very alien culture of formal church services. We've been using SU's Rooted resources, where we focus on key issues that are important to young people as a basis for discussion and Bible exploration.

Recently, I asked Francesca to tell me more about her thoughts on spirituality and the Christian faith. She said, 'I've believed in God from a young age. I've always tried to act as best I can towards others and to be kind. But it's only more recently through Recharge and Precharge that I've understood things like God and Jesus are separate but also one. And that Christianity isn't just about knowledge, it's about having faith. It surprised me a bit and I started asking questions.

'I enjoy reading the Bible because it tells me more about life, history and how I should live. After I went on SU's Quantum holiday, I was reading it every week and really enjoyed discussing it with Millie. Now I read it once every couple of months but want to read it more often (I just got out of the habit during the pandemic). I was given a Good News Bible as a leaver's gift by my primary school, and I use that.

'I like to pray – I try to pray every night before bed. I whisper rather than pray in my head, as it helps me to focus. I'm a bit in awe of God, like I would be of someone famous or important, but I also talk to him as a friend. I'm mostly open with him; tell him what's on my mind. I pray about family and friends – I might ask God to bless them, or for help with specific things. And I tell him what I'm thankful for.'

Faith Guides – providing direction and support

It's great that the groups I've helped to run, and SU's Quantum holiday, have developed Francesca's interest in reading the Bible and praying. But I think what's most revealing is her more recent discovery that being a Christian isn't just knowing about Jesus in your head, it's about believing in him in your

heart. If her faith journey had ended when primary school did, she may never have discovered that important truth for herself.

That's why Scripture Union is looking for volunteers to become Faith Guides, to walk with children and young people on their journey. You don't need to be a professional youth or children's worker to be a Faith Guide, and you can play an active part in helping the next generation to discover Jesus, explore faith and develop in their spiritual understanding.

Scripture Union will provide you with resources and training. Our Mission Enablers will mentor you and help you develop a vision for children and young people local to you, and support you to put your ideas into action.

So, if you feel that this is something to which God might be calling you, find out more about our new Revealing Jesus mission framework and becoming a Faith Guide at su.org.uk/revealingjesus.

A shorter version of this story first appeared in Connecting You, *SU's free quarterly supporter magazine. If you'd like to receive* Connecting You *and learn more of how God is moving in the hearts and lives of children and young people today, you can sign up online at su.org.uk/connectingyou or by calling 01908 856000.*

Dancing in the dark

It is now an established feature of election reporting that journalists accompany politicians on the campaign trail. Travelling at close quarters with party leaders and their team, news correspondents are able to provide 'fly on the wall' coverage of their efforts to engage voters. Unfortunately for the politicians, this means the cameras are still rolling, and the microphones still working, when they are confronted unexpectedly by members of the public asking awkward questions for which they have no pre-prepared answer. The result may delight viewers, but is often disastrous for the public image of the party and its representatives.

There is a sense in which Matthew 19-23 presents readers with dispatches from the frontline of Jesus' campaign to establish the kingdom of God on earth as it is in heaven, as it gathers momentum. Commencing in Judea but moving quickly to Jerusalem, where the campaign will reach its dramatic climax, these chapters allow us to journey 'up close and personal' with the Messiah as he encounters a variety of people, each with their own agenda and questions. Some are innocent and inquisitive, others calculating and malevolent.

Jesus, however, is never caught off guard. He is ready to respond to all who cross his path. Sometimes with compassion, sometimes with creativity, and sometimes with correction – and always with a wisdom that is utterly compelling. Continuing to speak truth to power, even as opposition to his kingdom-inaugurating campaign intensifies along the way, here is Jesus dancing in the dark.

About the writer
Nigel Hopper

An ordained Baptist minister, Nigel is currently a doctoral research student at the University of Birmingham, where he is investigating patterns of corvid distribution and abundance in the UK. He lives in Milton Keynes with his wife and two grown-up children.

The ties that bind

PREPARE

As a new year dawns, praise God for his past faithfulness and commit to trust him for all that lies ahead.

READ

Matthew 19:1–12

EXPLORE

Reading the possible side effects of the medication you've been prescribed by your doctor may make you wonder if you're better off not taking it at all! However, the fact that some people may experience a reaction doesn't detract from the fact that it was originally formulated, tested, and given to patients with the intention of making them better. Doctors would not want the relatively rare possibility of medication causing serious side effects to cause us to lose sight of its proven and established capacity to heal. In the same way, Jesus will not allow the tragic possibility of divorce in a fallen world to negate the fact that God's *intention* for marriage is that it is a lifelong, exclusive commitment (vs 4–6).

The Pharisees' question (v 3) is essentially focused on how far a person might move from God, in regard to marriage, without going too far. Jesus' response (vs 8,9) declares that the focus should be instead on how near a person might remain to God in working out their marital commitment. The reaction of the disciples to his teaching (v 10) was perhaps tongue-in-cheek, but Jesus uses it to make the serious – and countercultural – point that marriage *isn't* for everyone (v 11). In doing so, he endorses a life of celibate singleness as no less a gift than marriage.

> Jesus replied, 'Moses permitted you to divorce your wives because your hearts were hard. But it was not this way from the beginning.'

Matthew 19:8

RESPOND

What might Jesus' teaching about marriage mean for you personally, and for your support of others during this new year?

Bible in a year: Genesis 1,2; Matthew 1

Sunday 2 January
Psalm 27

Reason to believe

PREPARE
Recognising God's care for you, bring all your anxieties before him honestly now.

....

READ
Psalm 27

EXPLORE
There is dynamic interplay at work in this psalm, between confidence in God and seeking after God. The psalmist's confidence in God (v 1) drives him to seek God's presence (vs 4,7,8) which, in turn, serves to consolidate his confidence in God (vs 13,14). This affirmation of trust in God is occasioned by acute adversity – a matter of life or death (vs 2,3). The precise nature of the threat remains unspecified, so this psalm is appropriate for use in any circumstances that tempt us to surrender faith to fear.

The focus of God's presence for the psalmist is the Temple (vs 4,5). His prayer that God will come to his aid and guide him through the present crisis is set in the context of his desire to continue to be able to enjoy encountering the divine presence in the house of the Lord. However, this is not something the psalmist does in isolation. To talk of the Temple as he does is to reference the worship life of Israel. Trust and confidence in God are renewed here in community – and this psalm (like all psalms) was provided and preserved for community use.

In light of this, the worship life of our churches should be an essential means of seeking, and finding fresh confidence in God, doing so in honest acknowledgement of those terrors that threaten our trust in him.

> I remain confident of this: I will see the goodness of the LORD in the land of the living.
>
> **Psalm 27:13**

RESPOND
Meditate on Psalm 27:1. As you do so, note how emphasising different words affects its power and your understanding.

....

Bible in a year: Genesis 3,4; Matthew 2

Human touch

PREPARE

Recall your first conscious encounter with Christ; give thanks for those who introduced him to you.

....

READ

Matthew 19:13–15

EXPLORE

Matthew's narrative moves quite naturally from a discussion about marriage to the matter of children. It was not uncommon in Jesus' day for people to bring their children to a recognised holy man to receive his blessing. Why, then, were Jesus' disciples so reluctant to let the little children come to him (v 13)? We can only speculate, but the fact that beforehand they made no attempt to prevent the Pharisees coming to Jesus (v 3), and later on will do nothing to deter the approach of a rich man (v 16), suggests that they judged the children as unworthy of Christ's attention because they were powerless and insignificant. How might we effectively 'close off' Christ to people, as a result of blind adherence to the prevailing values and attitudes of our own societies?

Jesus' welcoming of the children is a wake-up call to his disciples. The kingdom of heaven operates according to a completely different value system from that which has governed their lives thus far; and they now need to live out kingdom principles. To this end, they need look no further than the children before them. Jesus not only has time for them, but also holds them up as a model of the attitude required to receive his rule and so enter into true discipleship (v 14).

> Jesus said, 'Let the little children come to me, and do not hinder them, for the kingdom of heaven belongs to such as these.'
>
> **Matthew 19:14**

RESPOND

What is it about children that makes them a model of those to whom God's kingdom belongs? Is there any area of life in which you need to become more childlike?

....

Bible in a year: Genesis 5,6; Matthew 3

Tuesday 4 January
Matthew 19:16–30

Hungry heart

PREPARE
Consider the many blessings you have received from God; praise him for his goodness.

READ
Matthew 19:16–30

EXPLORE
Normally, we come to the Bible eager to understand its meaning. However, when it comes to this passage, many of us may rush to state what it *doesn't* mean! Jesus, we console ourselves, doesn't call *all* those who follow him to surrender their wealth and possessions, just this particular individual (v 21). Our familiarity with these verses has perhaps bred contempt for the rich man – surely, one so wealthy could not possibly be disciple material. The judgment that someone else, because they have more money than we do, is more compromised in their commitment to Christ than we are, is all too easily made.

The disciples made the opposite assumption. Their astonishment at Jesus' assertion about how hard it is for the rich to enter the kingdom of heaven (v 25) indicates that they regarded this man as an ideal candidate for discipleship.

Both assumptions are wrong because neither leaves room for the goodness and grace of God. Entry into life in all its fullness rests not on human endeavour or material blessings, but in the hands of God. Since all things are possible with God (v 26), both rich and poor alike may attain the necessary detachment from wealth that permits complete devotion to Christ.

> Jesus ... said, 'With man this is impossible, but with God all things are possible.'
> **Matthew 19:26**

RESPOND
'That Jesus did not command all his followers to sell all their possessions gives comfort only to the kind of people to whom he would issue that command!'* Share your feelings about today's passage with God now.

*R. H. Gundry, *Matthew: A Commentary on His Literary and Theological Art*, Grand Rapids, Michigan, Wm. B. Eerdmans, 1982.

Bible in a year: Genesis 7,8; Psalms 1,2

My beautiful reward

PREPARE
Spend a few moments in wonder at your personal experience of God's grace.

READ
Matthew 20:1–16

EXPLORE

Grace isn't fair! That's the central point of this parable, told as an illustration of the kingdom principle that 'many who are first will be last, and many who are last will be first' (19:30; 20:16). This simple, but brilliantly crafted, story contributes to the education of the disciples in the 'new world order', which was arriving in and through Jesus' ministry. As listeners and readers, they and we are led to expect that those hired first to work in the vineyard will receive substantially more than those who were hired only late in the day. Then, to discover that all the workers receive the same wage (vs 9,10) seems like an outrage, at least from a secular employment point of view. The divine storyteller has very effectively teased out our inherent capacity for making God in our own image.

It's not that grace is unjust – all the hired workers received at least a fair wage – it's just that grace doesn't conform to the rules of a world where efforts dictate rewards. Rather, grace creates a new world. One in which a proper appreciation that each and every blessing flows forth from God's lavish generosity towards people who are all equally undeserving, leaves absolutely no room for disgruntled envy (v 15).

> 'Don't I have the right to do what I want with my own money? Or are you envious because I am generous?'
>
> **Matthew 20:15**

RESPOND
Bring before God those whom you (secretly) consider to be less deserving of his grace than you. Ask for his forgiveness, and for his help to become yourself an open channel of his grace to them.

Bible in a year: Genesis 9–11; Matthew 4

Thursday 6 January
Matthew 20:17–28

High hopes

PREPARE
If possible, kneel down and, in silence, focus on the fact that you are in the presence of God himself.

READ
Matthew 20:17–28

EXPLORE

There are occasions when certain programmes or films are pulled from television schedules because it is deemed inappropriate or insensitive to broadcast them given recent real-life events. In light of his recent teaching on kingdom values, Jesus might well have hoped that James and John (and their mother) would have 'pulled' their request to secure the 'best seats in the house' (v 21). Their petition is all the more insensitive and inappropriate coming as it does after Jesus predicts – for the third time in Matthew's Gospel – his own suffering and death (vs 18,19). Jesus may be a great teacher, but his disciples are hardly model pupils.

Yet how graciously Jesus deals with this most incongruous of requests – accepting it as an honest expression of naivety rather than a wilful denial of his teaching (v 22). Truly, God knows us better than we know ourselves.

The reaction of the other disciples (v 24) speaks more of envy of the brothers' bold initiative than it does of their own embrace of kingdom principles. What all twelve, and all who would follow Jesus after them, *must* learn is that the way of discipleship really is the way of Christ himself (vs 25–28). God will advance his kingdom on earth as it was inaugurated – through humble service and sacrifice.

> '… whoever wants to become great among you must be your servant.'
>
> **Matthew 20:26**

RESPOND
Think of all the different areas of life in which you hold some kind of authority. How does your exercise of that authority reflect kingdom principles?

Bible in a year: Genesis 12,13; Matthew 5

Eyes on the prize

PREPARE
Pray that you would encounter God powerfully through his Word now.

• •

READ
Matthew 20:29–34

EXPLORE
Susan Boyle is now an internationally acclaimed singing star. However, back in 2009 when she first auditioned for a British television talent show, her stated ambition of becoming a professional singer was met with derision. Before she had even sung a note, she had been written off as having no hope of realising her dream – presumably because of her appearance.

Something like that happens to the two blind men sitting by the road out of Jericho. Their attempt to attract the attention of Jesus (v 30) is met with contempt from the accompanying crowd (v 31), some of whom may well have tossed a couple of coins their way to 'buy their silence', having judged that money must be all that these social outcasts were after. Jesus, however, hears something more in their persistent cries – nothing less than a faith that literally stops him in his tracks (v 32).

Though blind, these beggars already see Jesus – whom they address as God's Messiah – as the one who can restore their sight (v 33). Jesus' question to them is not to nurture a previously absent faith, but to tease out their existing faith for the benefit of the crowd that had written them off.

Contrary to appearances, these men are model disciples who ask in faith, according to kingdom priorities, and so receive just as Jesus promised (Matthew 7:7,8).

> Jesus stopped and called them. 'What do you want me to do for you?' he asked.
>
> **Matthew 20:32**

RESPOND
Who are you tempted to write off as lacking saving faith? How might you use questions to discover more about their experience of God?

• •

Bible in a year: Genesis 14,15; Psalms 3,4

Saturday 8 January
Matthew 21:1–11

Land of hope and dreams

PREPARE
Sing or speak a song of praise to Jesus as king.

....

READ
Matthew 21:1–11

EXPLORE

'If it looks like a duck, swims like a duck, and quacks like a duck, then it probably *is* a duck!' According to this reasoning, Jesus' entry into Jerusalem must be understood as a royal drama. Christ's use of a donkey to enact the prophecy of Zechariah 9:9 (vs 4,5), the crowd spreading their cloaks on the ground before him, waving leafy branches (v 8), shouting praise from Psalm 118 (a royal psalm), and addressing Jesus with the Messianic title, 'Son of David' (v 9), all testify to this being the moment when God's long-promised king arrives to save his people and establish his reign in the Holy City. Matthew would be very happy for his readers, after these verses, to arrive at the conclusion that Jesus is king.

Acknowledging Jesus as king is one thing; understanding and accepting his style of kingship is quite another (it is one thing to identify a duck, quite another to tell individual species of duck apart!). The jubilation of the crowd suggests that they rightly had expectations of liberation but, wrongly, no comprehension that the Christ would ascend to his throne through suffering and sacrifice – thereby setting the pattern of life for all who would subsequently call themselves Christians. Accepting Jesus as king requires that we liberate him from the confines of our expectations and actually submit to his reign.

> When Jesus entered Jerusalem, the whole city was stirred and asked, 'Who is this?'
>
> **Matthew 21:10**

RESPOND
Use Psalm 118 as a basis for celebrating God's faithfulness and the good news of what he has done in Jesus.

....

Bible in a year: Genesis 16,17; Matthew 6

Lift me up

PREPARE
Take time to delight in God, and your experiences of him answering your prayers.

....

READ
Psalm 28

EXPLORE
If we truly trust God, then we must allow him a free hand; the subtext of all our prayers must be 'your will be done, on earth as it is in heaven'. It is this confidence that is on display in Psalm 28 – a prayer offered in the midst of a personal situation so desperate that the psalmist likens it to a journey down into the realm of the dead (v 1). That, it is envisaged, will be the deserved fate of his enemies – even so the psalmist pleads for God to act according to his justice and faithfulness (vs 3–5). Even in desperation, judgment is deferred to God.

The sudden move from desperation to delight in the psalm (v 6) does not necessarily presuppose the resolution of the crisis. Rather, it presupposes that the prayer offered as an act of faith in the darkness *has been heard by God*. That fact alone is enough to assure the psalmist of divine assistance, and so is cause for joyous celebration in the company of God's covenant people, even before the nature of divine aid has been revealed (vs 7,8,9). In total trust that he has been heard, the psalmist leaves God free to answer as he sees fit. The character and faithfulness of God mean that praise, like prayer, is appropriate even in the eye of the storm.

The LORD is my strength and my shield; my heart trusts in him, and he helps me.
Psalm 28:7a

RESPOND
Tell God about anything that is distressing you. Consider his faithfulness, then praise him in joyous anticipation of his help.

....

Bible in a year: Genesis 18,19; Matthew 7

Monday 10 January
Matthew 21:12–22

My father's house

PREPARE
Ask God to open your heart and your mind to what he has to say to you now.

· ·

READ
Matthew 21:12–22

EXPLORE
One of the reasons adults enjoy the *Toy Story* films as much as children is their deliberate referencing of classic lines and scenes from iconic movies. Awareness of this opens up additional levels of appreciation of the films.

Similarly, to fully appreciate the significance of Jesus' actions in these verses, readers need to be familiar with the Old Testament stories and prophecies referenced in them. Jesus' clearing of an area in the Temple courts (vs 12,13) enacts the prophecy of Zechariah 14:21, even as he quotes from Isaiah (56:7) and Jeremiah (7:11). His welcoming and healing of the blind and the lame to the Temple (v 14) counters the policy of exclusion that had been in place since the time of David (2 Samuel 5:8). And the cursing of a fruitless fig tree (v 19) recalls various Old Testament references concerned with the inevitability of the judgement of fruitless Israel, not least Micah 7:1–6.

Jesus' actions and words declare that 'time is up' for Israel, that judgement is imminent and will result in the Temple itself being rendered redundant. Would God's people set aside cherished traditions, and embrace Jesus as the ultimate fulfilment of God's promises? A question as relevant for us now as it was for the people of Jerusalem back then.

> Seeing a fig-tree ... he went up to it but found nothing on it except leaves. Then he said to it, 'May you never bear fruit again!' Immediately the tree withered.
> **Matthew 21:19**

RESPOND
What are your habits of spiritual formation? What changes this year might result in greater fruitfulness?

· ·

Bible in a year: Genesis 20,21; Matthew 8

Hearts of stone

PREPARE
Meditate on Proverbs 2:6. Keep this verse in mind as you go on to encounter Jesus in Matthew's Gospel today.

READ
Matthew 21:23–27

EXPLORE
'Just answer the question!' How many times have you said or thought that as you watched or listened to a politician respond to an interviewer's question with anything but a direct answer? You could be forgiven for thinking that Jesus is attempting to evade the question put to him here by the chief priests and elders, but his interrogators wouldn't have seen it that way. Responding to one question with another, to elucidate more precisely the matter in hand, was common practice in first-century rabbinic circles.

The focus of the debate is authority (v 23). Jesus' actions on arrival in Jerusalem had asserted his own authority and, therefore, challenged the authority of the Jewish religious leaders. Understandably, they wanted the upstart rabbi to lay out his credentials. Their question immediately betrays their conviction that Jesus has no authority, and so reveals their spiritual blindness.

Christ's counterquestion (vs 24–25) exposes the hard-heartedness of his inquisitors. Since they refused to accept John the Baptist as a prophet acting under God's authority (vs 25–26), they are hardly ready to recognise the authority of Jesus whom John publicly endorsed as God's Messiah through baptism (John 1:29–34). So, there is little point in Jesus answering their question (v 27). Here is the wisdom of God at work to disarm deceit.

> Jesus replied, 'I will also ask you one question. If you answer me, I will tell you by what authority I am doing these things.'
> **Matthew 21:24**

RESPOND
Ask God to help you grow in wisdom, and to give you the courage to exercise that wisdom in all things.

Bible in a year: Genesis 22,23; Psalms 5,6

Worlds apart

PREPARE

What convinced you to believe the good news of what God has done in Jesus? Praise him for his gracious intervention in your life.

READ

Matthew 21:28–32

EXPLORE

Having already disarmed deceit, here is the wisdom of God at work to disclose the truth. By feigning ignorance in response to Jesus' question concerning John's baptism (21:27), the chief priests and elders had attempted to conceal their rejection of John in order to 'save face' among the people. Knowing this, Jesus invites their judgment on the matter of two fictional sons who respond differently to their father's request to go and work in the family vineyard. In contrast to their previous reticence, the religious leaders declare instantly which son they believe to be in the right (v 31). In doing so, they show themselves to be in the wrong in regard to John (v 32) – and, by extension, to Jesus also.

Contrary to their own expectations, it is *not* the chief priests and elders who are represented by the son whom they judge to have done the father's will in Jesus' story. It is tax collectors and prostitutes (v 31)! When it came to recognising what God was doing and getting on board with it, the religious leaders were lagging far behind those whom they considered farthest from God (v 32). This, of course, could never happen today in our churches, could it?

> Jesus said to them, 'Truly I tell you, the tax collectors and the prostitutes are entering the kingdom of God ahead of you.'
>
> **Matthew 21:31b**

RESPOND

How can you ensure that your own desire to be discerning about claims of God's activity in the world does not translate into unbelief?

Bible in a year: Genesis 24,25; Matthew 9

Wages of sin

PREPARE

Invite the Holy Spirit to work in you now, to grow you in both faith and fruitfulness.

- -

READ

Matthew 21:33–46

EXPLORE

If you rent out your house, you expect the tenants to look after your property. If they fail to do so, you will end the agreement and find new tenants who will take proper care of what belongs to you. Essentially, the same principle applies to God and his dealings with his people.

Deliberately evoking the imagery of Isaiah 5:1–7, Jesus' story speaks of Israel's historical mistreatment of the prophets (vs 35–36), and her impending rejection of him (vs 37–39). This is a people that has failed to bear the fruit required by God, and of religious leaders, who – especially culpable for this failure – will have their tenancy terminated (v 43). Fruitlessness is not without consequences.

However, there's something more than régime change here. God is going to renew the whole 'house' of his people to fulfil their covenant calling to be a light to the nations – all through Jesus, the Messiah, and his disciples! He is the once-rejected but resurrected Son in whom God's people will hold together (vs 39,42). He is also the stone that will ultimately crush all kingdoms that refuse to submit to his reign (v 44) – including that which the chief priests and Pharisees had built for themselves around the Temple and its traditions. Fruitlessness is not without consequences.

> 'Therefore I tell you that the kingdom of God will be taken away from you and given to a people who will produce its fruit.'

Matthew 21:43

RESPOND

Reflect on Jesus' description of himself in verse 44. Might this change your view of Jesus and his kingship?

- -

Bible in a year: Genesis 26,27; Matthew 10

Living proof

PREPARE
Give thanks for your entry into God's kingdom through Christ.

· ·

READ
Matthew 22:1–14

EXPLORE
Now, be honest, we weren't expecting that, were we? There we were, reading Jesus' story about a wedding banquet, happily spotting the allegories – Israel's rejection of her Messiah (vs 4–5), God's impending judgement on his people (v 7), his embrace of ordinary people like us (vs 8–10) – and then it's all ruined by the unpleasant business with the man who is dressed inappropriately for the occasion (vs 11–13). What is going on?

It's a stark warning from Jesus that fruitfulness is no less important for the renewed people of God than it had been for the Old Testament people of Israel (remember the vineyard). The wedding clothes in the parable are an allegory for fruitfulness, and it is fruitfulness that distinguishes the chosen from the invited (v 14). The man thrown out of the banquet had failed to dress in a manner befitting the occasion – he didn't really belong there. In the same way, if our lives are not 'clothed' in kingdom values then we give ourselves away as not belonging in the kingdom of God.

We can make much of our being saved by faith alone. Here is a powerful reminder that we are saved for the purpose of fruitfulness – of demonstrating the goodness of living under the reign of Christ.

> He asked, 'How did you get in here without wedding clothes, friend?'
>
> **Matthew 22:12**

RESPOND
Talk to God about areas of your life in which you have been content to conform rather than to live fruitfully. Ask for his help in growing the 'obedience that comes from faith' (Romans 1:5).

· ·

Bible in a year: Genesis 28,29; Psalms 7,8

Pay me my money down

PREPARE

Praise and worship God for his creation and reflect before him on what it means for you to be made in his image (Genesis 1:27).

READ

Matthew 22:15–22

EXPLORE

Quite apart from anything else, this encounter demonstrates the futility of pretending before God. Jesus sees straight through the feigned praise of the Pharisees and Herodians (v 16) and exposes their hypocrisy not only verbally (v 18), but also visually.

By inviting his questioners to produce a denarius (v 19), Jesus forces them to reveal that they carry about their person Roman currency. This was held by the Jews to be idolatrous on account of the coins bearing the image of the emperor and an inscription declaring him to be both a divine son and high priest. Suddenly, those who came to trap Jesus as an enemy of the state look suspiciously like friends of Rome and therefore opponents of God. Jesus, however, has no objection to paying the poll-tax; to do so is to give back to Caesar what is due to Caesar (v 21), with no suggestion that the payment in any way compromises devotion to God. We therefore need to consider very carefully under what circumstances might civil disobedience be sometimes a faithful expression, and sometimes a failure, of true worship.

God must also be given what is due to him (v 21). In the immediate context this likely refers to the fruit of obedience, including that of accepting and submitting to Jesus as Messiah and Lord.

… 'So give back to Caesar what is Caesar's, and to God what is God's.'

Matthew 22:21b

RESPOND

How might Jesus' teaching here inform Christian action to address contemporary political and societal issues (eg climate change; systemic racial, ethnic, gender and other unconscious bias)?

Sunday 16 January
Psalm 29

No surrender

PREPARE
Call to mind your favourite hymn or worship song. Focus on the truths it teaches about your God.

READ
Psalm 29

EXPLORE

Have you ever thought that singing praise to God is an act of defiance? That realisation only really struck me during the thanksgiving service for the life of my dad. Our tears and sadness at his untimely death were real, but through them we sang of the hope we had because of what God has done in Christ. Our songs were not an exercise in denial, but in defiance. To sing of the reality of God, and of what he has done, is to insist that there is one more powerful than the pain and darkness that seem so often to prevail in our world.

Psalm 29 is a gift of a song with which to express faithful defiance in a fallen world. It plays to the rhythm of a ferocious thunderstorm in which the powerful voice of God is heard (vs 3–5,7– 9), and his majestic, incomparable power is displayed (vs 5–9). This is in direct defiance of the Canaanite god, Baal, whose worshippers held that his voice was heard in the storm. Indeed, it may well be that this psalm is the result of an idolatrous hymn of praise having been purposefully reworked into a song celebrating the one true God. Redeeming culture is one of the ways in which God's people on earth can echo his praise in the heavens (vs 1,9).

> The voice of the LORD twists the oaks and strips the forest bare. And in his temple all cry, 'Glory!'

Psalm 29:9

RESPOND
Sing a hymn of praise to God, acknowledging that you are engaging in an act of faithful defiance.

Bible in a year: Genesis 32,33; Matthew 12

The rising

PREPARE
Personalise the words of Ephesians 1:18–21 as you prepare to meet with God through his Word.

READ
Matthew 22:23–33

EXPLORE

We don't often think of Jesus agreeing with the Pharisees, but he did agree with them about the reality of the resurrection. The Sadducees, however, did not. The farcical scenario they present to Jesus here (vs 25–28) is intended to use the law of Moses to make a mockery of his belief in the resurrection. Imagine their reaction then, when Jesus states that their question makes a mockery of their knowledge both of the Scriptures and of the power of God (v 29)!

In regard to the power of God, the Sadducees fail to appreciate that at the resurrection God will transform and renew all things – including human beings – making marriage unnecessary in the new creation (v 30). With regard to the Scriptures, they have failed to see that God's introduction of himself to Moses at the burning bush – where he speaks of the dead patriarchs as though they were living – presupposes the reality of resurrection (vs 31,32).

Again, the wisdom of God is at work in Jesus, to counter and correct. The pattern of his response to the Sadducees suggests a pattern for our own experience of God. The greater our familiarity with Scripture, the greater our familiarity with the God who is revealed therein. The greater our familiarity with God, the greater our awareness of his power.

> Jesus replied, 'You are in error because you do not know the Scriptures or the power of God.'
> **Matthew 22:29**

RESPOND
Thank God for your past experience of his resurrection power. Ask him to act in those situations where you long to see that at work in the present.

Bible in a year: Genesis 34–36; Matthew 13

Tuesday 18 January
Matthew 22:34–46

Blinded by the light

PREPARE
Use the words of Psalm 113 to help focus your thoughts on God now.

. . . .

READ
Matthew 22:34–46

EXPLORE
Like tag team wrestlers the Pharisees take over from the defeated Sadducees and 'step into the ring' to spar verbally with Jesus once more. His identification of love as the lens through which to understand and live the commands of the Old Testament (vs 37–40) inspires neither antagonism nor amazement – it is evidently an entirely orthodox answer. Jesus has no interest in being controversial for its own sake. He is only ever caught up in controversy when the kingdoms of this world resist the claims of the kingdom of heaven issued through his ministry. The same should surely hold true for the church as it continues Christ's mission today.

At the heart of that mission, of course, is the declaration that, in Jesus, God entered into the world and acted to save and renew his creation. Jesus is the Messiah; he is David's son; but more than that, he is the Son of God! That's what he's driving at with his question to the Pharisees concerning the sonship of the Messiah (v 42). The title 'son of David' is good so far as it goes, but it doesn't go far enough (v 45); it fails to do sufficient justice to the full significance of Christ. The mission of the church must do full justice to Jesus.

> 'What do you think about the Messiah? Whose son is he?'
>
> **Matthew 22:42a**

RESPOND
Look up some of the many different biblical titles for the Messiah, eg Son of God, servant, king. Spend a few moments reflecting on each individually. What do they convey to you about Jesus?

. . . .

Bible in a year: Genesis 37,38; Psalm 9

Brilliant disguise

PREPARE

Picture Jesus washing the feet of his disciples (John 13:1–17). What is it about this scene that attracts you to Christ?

READ

Matthew 23:1–12

EXPLORE

During the course of the COVID-19 pandemic, a number of politicians in the UK were forced to apologise – even resign – when it emerged that they had breached the restrictions they had imposed to limit the spread of the virus. The charge levelled at them by the media was that of hypocrisy – national leaders demonstrating by their behaviour that they were unwilling to live by the rules they had enforced on the general public.

That's precisely how Jesus describes the conduct of the Pharisees here, as he warns his hearers against following their example (v 3). Their hypocrisy is rooted in a desire for prestige and status that governs their appearance, social life, and preferred salutations (vs 5–7). It is love for self, rather than whole-life love for God and neighbour, that serves as their primary motivation.

In stark contrast, Jesus requires that humility be the defining characteristic of the Christian community. Recognising God as Father, Jesus as Messiah, and fellow believers as sisters and brothers, the church must resist self-promoting status structures from wider society (vs 8–10). The kingdom of heaven ushers in a whole new world order, not merely a spiritual rebranding of the *status quo*. We must demonstrate to our celebrity-obsessed world that we take Christ at his word – that service is the way of greatness (v 11).

'The greatest among you will be your servant.'

Matthew 23:11

RESPOND

How might Jesus' teaching in these verses inform guidelines for the use of social media by Christians and churches?

Bible in a year: Genesis 39,40; Matthew 14

Thursday 20 January

Matthew 23:13–39

Two faces

PREPARE
'Search me, God, and know my heart ... See if there is any offensive way in me...'
(Psalm 139:23–24).

READ
Matthew 23:13–39

EXPLORE
This detailed exposé of the hypocrisy of the Pharisees is a blistering attack by Jesus. He pulls no punches as he lays out the evidence for his earlier charge that they fail to practise what they preach (23:3). So consumed have they become with the tiniest details of the application of the Law that they have completely lost sight of its intended purpose – to produce the fruit of a life orientated towards love for God and neighbour. Their heart is in the wrong place. If only it were in the right place, then many of the outer details over which they agonise would take care of themselves. That the gaping inconsistency between the Pharisees' ritual posturing and the reality of their relationship with God should provoke such harsh criticism from Jesus, should give us pause for thought.

Christ's words, however, are not motivated by hatred; his own heart is well and truly in the right place. Read again the arresting maternal imagery he uses to describe his ministry to Jerusalem (v 37). He feels keenly his responsibility for the salvation of his people, and so feels equally keenly the pain of their rejection of him, for which they must take responsibility (v 38). Anger that is genuinely righteous arises not from wounded pride, but from a broken heart.

'Jerusalem, Jerusalem ... how often I have longed to gather your children together, as a hen gathers her chicks under her wings, and you were not willing.'
Matthew 23:37

RESPOND
Meditate on Jesus' words in verse 37. What do these convey to you about God, and the expression of his love in Jesus?

Bible in a year: Genesis 41,42; Matthew 15

REVEALING
JESUS

Revealing Jesus is a new mission framework from Scripture Union, designed to help you journey into faith with the **95%** of children and young people not in church.

FIND OUT MORE: SU.ORG.UK/REVEALINGJESUS

Pilgrims on the way

Getting ready for a long journey takes time! What clothes to take? Is everyone ready to go?

Numbers comes at a pivotal point in the story of God's people. God has rescued them from slavery in Egypt. They have arrived at Mount Sinai and God has provided for their needs both physical and spiritual. They have a covenant law to live by (Exodus 19,20), a tent of meeting for worship (Exodus 35–40), and rituals to ensure their sins are forgiven (Leviticus 1–27).

In Numbers, we see the pilgrims finally ready for their journey to the land of Canaan. We will read of their preparations for departure (chapters 1–10), their setting out on the way (chapters 10–12), the challenges and setbacks that face them (chapters 13–19), and finally their arrival in Moab with the promised land just in sight (chapters 20–36). Along the way the people learn lessons about holy living, the importance of leadership, the dangers of temptation, and how God is ever gracious and faithful to his promises.

As you read these early chapters of the book, look out for new insights that God will give you. Explore your own pilgrimage of faith and consider what it means to live for the God who still journeys alongside us today. Why? For in the words of the apostle Paul: '…these things occurred as examples *for us*' (1 Corinthians 10:6, NRSVA). So, from one pilgrim to another: enjoy the adventure!

About the writer
Richard Trist

Richard is the Dean of the Anglican Institute at Ridley College in Melbourne, Australia. He served for many years in parish ministry, and now enjoys training future leaders and pastors. He is married to Glenda, a hospital pastoral care worker. In his spare time, he enjoys reading, movies and travel.

Holy God, holy people

PREPARE

Think of some of the ways in which you serve God in the church and the world. Thank God for this privilege.

READ

Numbers 3:1–16

EXPLORE

The pilgrims are preparing to travel (see Numbers 1–2). Fighting men are counted. Tribes are arranged in the camp. The tribe of Levi is counted for a different purpose. Their job is to support the priests in maintaining the tabernacle (v 7). They have been especially set apart in place of Israel's firstborn (vs 12,13).

Yet the privilege of serving God comes with responsibility. He is a holy God. Being a Levite or even a son of Aaron does not guarantee protection if wrong attitudes lead to sinful actions (v 4). Beware of messing with God or he might mess with you!

As Christians, we can be thankful that the warning of verse 10 no longer applies. Why? 'We have confidence to enter the Most Holy Place by the blood of Jesus' (Hebrews 10:19). Freely coming to God is possible, serving him becomes a joy. Yet such service must be curated with care. Even the best of our efforts can be spoiled if driven by selfish motives. Like the Levites we must ensure our lives are given 'wholly to him' (v 9).

> 'Give the Levites to Aaron and his sons; they are the Israelites who are to be given wholly to him.'
>
> **Numbers 3:9**

RESPOND:

Pray (or sing) these words from this hymn: 'All to Jesus I surrender, all to him I freely give; / I will ever love and trust him, / In his presence daily live. / I surrender all.'* What will this mean for you as you serve God today?

*Judson W. Van de Venter (1855–1939).

Bible in a year: Genesis 43,44; Psalm 10

Numbers 4:1–28

All have a part to play

PREPARE
'The law of the LORD is perfect, refreshing the soul' (Psalm 19:7). Ask God to do this today by his Word.

....

READ
Numbers 4:1–28

EXPLORE
In most workplaces, including churches, clear job descriptions ensure everyone knows what needs to be done. It is not enough to simply 'hope for the best'.

Such care is seen when the Israelites begin their onward journey. Everybody has a role. The priests have special responsibility to pack up the tabernacle: curtains are taken down, plates and bowls wrapped, the golden altar covered (vs 5–14). The Kohathites carry the ark of the covenant and the holy utensils. This task comes with a warning. Carelessly touching the things of God will bring instant judgement (v 15). The Gershonites have their own responsibilities. They will carry the outer parts of the tabernacle using oxen (see 7:6–9). And for the rest of Israel? Most serve in the army to attack and defend when needed (1:45–46).

Here is a vivid reminder of the biblical principle that all have a part to play in serving God. He is sovereignly working out his plan, but everyone has a task. Each must cooperate with others to reach the final goal.

What about us? Every member of Christ's body has been given a gift or a cluster of gifts from the Holy Spirit 'for the common good' (1 Corinthians 12:7). Serving, leading, teaching, praying, and more. It is as we exercise these gifts that we move forward together as God's pilgrim people to reach our heavenly home.

> Aaron and his sons are to go into the sanctuary and assign to each man his work and what he is to carry.
>
> **Numbers 4:19**

RESPOND
Do you know your gifts? How can you exercise them today?

....

Bible in a year: Genesis 45,46; Matthew 16

From peril to praise

PREPARE
Recall people you know whose faith has grown despite suffering. Give thanks and pray for them.

....

READ
Psalm 30

EXPLORE
This psalm recounts a time when King David was close to death. Life had been good for him, and he felt sure and secure (v 6). Yet in retrospect he recognises that he had been overconfident. An all-too-common experience, the pride that comes before a fall (Proverbs 16:18).

Although details are scarce, David may have had a life-threatening illness (v 2). A family member's recent experience with cancer is a reminder that periods like these are never easy. At such times, God's presence can feel far away (v 7).

God hears David's prayer, and he is spared (v 3). As a result, he cannot be silent but sings the praises of God (v 12). What an amazing God! He turns weeping into joy, wailing into dancing (vs 5,11). David calls others to recognise the goodness of God (v 4). His deliverance does not just affect him – it affects all who hear about it. The power of testimony!

This prayer models for us how to respond when healing comes after illness – praise, thanksgiving, telling others the good news. It also points to God's greater work of dealing with human suffering through the death and resurrection of Jesus. Even as we suffer 'for a little while', we know God ultimately triumphs (1 Peter 1:3–7).

You turned my wailing into dancing; you removed my sackcloth and clothed me with joy.

Psalm 30:11

RESPOND
Consider how God has worked in your life. Is there someone you can share this with in the coming week?

....

Bible in a year: Genesis 47,48; Matthew 17

Monday 24 January
Numbers 5:1–31

Relationships matter

PREPARE
Reflect on a time when you were wronged in a relationship. What was its impact on you and others?

. . . .

READ
Numbers 5:1–31

EXPLORE
For Israel to live out their calling as God's holy people, right relationships were vital. Moses spells out just what this means. Clear but challenging guidelines are given.

The first relates to purity within the camp. Potential dangers are highlighted – infectious skin diseases, bodily discharges, a decaying body (v 2). The remedy is social distancing (v 3) – not a recent invention! The second set of guidelines deals with unethical financial dealings. If you break promises to others you are being unfaithful to me, says the Lord (v 6). Confession followed by generous restitution must occur (v 7).

Finally, the importance of faithfulness in marriage (vs 12–31). How quickly jealousy and suspicion arise when trust is eroded. The ceremony described seems strange to us but ultimately ensures that truth prevails. In a world with few rights for women, innocent wives are protected

from 'the inevitable bias of the male dominated trial'.* God alone can be trusted to be fair. He will guarantee justice be done.

If we are to be salt and light in the world, right relationships amongst God's people are vital (Matthew 5:13–16). Supporting marriages to be faithful and encouraging integrity in financial affairs are practical ways in which we can do this. What might this look like in your church community?

> Say to the Israelites, 'Any man or woman who wrongs another in any way and so is unfaithful to the LORD is guilty.'
> **Numbers 5:6**

RESPOND
Pray for any broken relationships you know of in your church – for truth and grace to prevail.

*Roy Gane, *Leviticus, Numbers*, NIV Application Commentary series, Zondervan, p525.

. . . .

Bible in a year: Genesis 49,50; Matthew 18

A life of dedication

PREPARE
Where are you most challenged as a disciple of Jesus? Bring this to God in prayer.

. . . .

READ
Numbers 6:1–21

EXPLORE
The public making of a vow is a solemn but joyful occasion. A bride and groom exchanging wedding rings. An elected official swearing allegiance on the Bible. New arrivals at a citizenship ceremony. Each occasion is a time of hope, with fresh responsibilities given and made.

For God's people, the Nazirite vow was an opportunity for any Israelite to express their dedication to the Lord and offer special service and commitment (v 2). Unlike priests and Levites, who were called by God to serve him, Nazirites were those who *voluntarily* set themselves aside for the Lord.* This was a personal choice. An outward response to an inner conviction. Note the visible signs. No more alcohol (v 3). Hair not to be cut (v 5). Contact with the dead avoided (v 6). If the latter occurred, provision was made for rededication (vs 9–20). This was no light and easy commitment.

*The Hebrew word *nazir* means set apart.

Like the Nazirites, some Christians may choose special times of dedication to God, such as prayer and fasting. Jesus commends this but challenges us to be aware of human pride (Matthew 6:5–18). What ultimately counts is the day-to-day living out of our faith, offering our whole lives to God 'as a living sacrifice, holy and pleasing to God' (Romans 12:1).

This is the law of the Nazirite … They must fulfil the vows they have made.
Numbers 6:21

RESPOND
Has God recently convicted you of something in your life of discipleship? How can you put this into practice?

. . . .

Bible in a year: Exodus 1,2; Psalms 11,12

Wednesday 26 January
Numbers 6:22–7:11

Blessings abundant

PREPARE
Take time to praise God for blessing us 'with every spiritual blessing in Christ' (Ephesians 1:3).

READ
Numbers 6:22–7:11

EXPLORE

Pilgrimages can be tiring. Early mornings and long distances lead to weary travellers. In leading tours of the Holy Land, I have found it is so important to start each day's journey with a group devotion and a prayer. Tired eyes soon begin to spark up. Today's adventure begins.

With Israel's journey about to begin, God gives Aaron and the priests such a start to their day, a blessing to help them on their way (vs 24–26). Look at each line carefully. Notice how each describes the Lord's promises of how he will act towards his people. He will bless them and keep them (v 24). With danger ahead he guarantees their protection and future. He then assures them of his love and grace (v 25). As a parent's face lights up when they see their newborn child, so the Lord's face constantly shines with pleasure towards Israel his son (Jeremiah 31:20). Finally, he pledges his presence and peace (v 26). God's constant attention will assuredly lead to *shalom* – Israel's well-being, health and prosperity.

In the light of this, the response of the people is unsurprising. Tribe after tribe bring a fellowship offering to be dedicated at the altar (vs 10,11,17). The people recognise that God's generosity deserves nothing less.

> 'So they will put my name on the Israelites, and I will bless them.'
>
> **Numbers 6:27**

RESPOND
Although Aaron's prayer of blessing is prayed corporately, the words are addressed to individuals. What do you need to hear from it today?

Bible in a year: Exodus 3,4; Matthew 19

Partners in the work

PREPARE

Think of your church and all those involved in 'behind the scenes' work – cleaners, caterers, administrators, pastoral carers. Give thanks for each one involved and the contribution they make.

READ

Numbers 7:89–8:26

EXPLORE

The Israelite camp has been set in order. God is with his people. Preparations commence for worship. First the setting up of lamps in the tabernacle (vs 1–4). Light for the priests as they do their work. Next, the dedication of the Levites. They are ceremonially cleansed (vs 5–7), then set apart by the laying on of hands (v 10). The Levites are to take the place of the firstborn Israelites in serving God at the sanctuary (v 18). They are God's 'gifts' to Aaron and his fellow priests (v 19).

For busy priests, burdened with the work of offering daily sacrifices, the support of the Levites was vital. Time-consuming duties made easier by their faithful service. It is still the case today. All churches today need people such as this, willing to take on 'backroom' tasks enabling pastors to focus on ministries of word and prayer (Acts 6:4). Paul speaks of such people as partners in the gospel (Philippians 1:5). For them it is not about being in the limelight but, like the Levites, simply the privilege of doing God's work whatever it might be.

> 'Present the Levites before the LORD as a wave offering from the Israelites, so that they may be ready to do the work of the LORD.'
>
> **Numbers 8:11**

RESPOND

A wise minister once told me: 'People come to church for all sorts of reasons but only stay for two – roles and relationships.' What roles are currently needed in your church family? Who can you encourage to be involved?

Bible in a year: Exodus 5,6; Matthew 20

The God who guides

PREPARE
Reflect on your own Christian journey and how God has guided you along the way. What patterns do you see?

READ
Numbers 9:1–23

EXPLORE
It is now 12 months since Israel was rescued from the judgement that passed over homes in Egypt (v 1). The time has come to celebrate God's miraculous deliverance in the Passover festival. Questions arise about participants. Those who have cared for a dying relative (v 7). Foreigners living amongst them. The answers are uncomplicated. The festival can be celebrated a month later (vs 10,11). Foreigners are welcome to join in (v 14).

But what about the future? God reassures the people of his continued presence in the cloud covering the tabernacle. The way ahead may be unclear, but he will show them when they should move on and when they should settle (v 17). Note the number of times we read of 'the Lord's command' (vs 18,19,20,23). The key thing for Israel is to trust in God and obey his guidance.

Most Christians experience times when we are bewildered by a lack of God's guidance. We wonder if he has forgotten us. We struggle to hold on. Yet as one commentator notes, 'Waiting times are not wasted times'.* We can use such times to continue to trust in God. He is ever present with us.

> Whenever the cloud lifted from above the tent, the Israelites set out; wherever the cloud settled, the Israelites set up camp.
>
> **Numbers 9:17**

RESPOND
Ponder this promise: 'Trust in the LORD with all your heart … in all your ways submit to him, and he will make your paths straight' (Proverbs 3:5,6).

*Raymond Brown, *The Message of Numbers*, Bible Speaks Today series, IVP, 2002, p75.

Bible in a year: Exodus 7,8; Psalms 13,14

The journey begins

PREPARE

'Be still, and know that I am God' (Psalm 46:10). Take time to put away concerns and worries. Remember the One who is in control.

READ

Numbers 10:1–13, 33–36

EXPLORE

God's final instructions to Moses at Mount Sinai are to make two trumpets. These will declare that God's army is ready and on the move. They will call leaders together (v 4), coordinate the tribes as they move (vs 5,6), and sound the attack in battle (v 9).

What mixed feelings the Israelites must have had as they set out (v 12,13). Excitement and elation, but perhaps also anxiety and fear. Are we ready for this? Will we manage what lies ahead? Moses' words give reassurance (v 35). The King of kings is in command. Planning and leadership are vital. But what matters most is the God who leads them. Though the journey is hard, Moses knows that God will keep his promise to Abraham, to give his people a land (Genesis 15:18–21).

The New Testament reminds us that we, too, are on a journey. We look for the city that is to come (Hebrews 13:14). Like Israel, the way ahead will not be easy, but we have One who has gone ahead. 'Let us run with perseverance the race marked out for us, fixing our eyes on Jesus...' (Hebrews 12:1,2). What will keep your eyes fixed upon him today?

> They set out from the mountain of the LORD and travelled for three days. The ark of the covenant of the LORD went before them ... to find them a place to rest.
>
> **Numbers 10:33**

RESPOND

On the last day, God's people will again be summoned 'with a loud trumpet call' and the dead raised 'imperishable' (Matthew 24:31; 1 Corinthians 15:52). Reflect and give thanks.

Bible in a year: Exodus 9,10; Matthew 21

What defines me

PREPARE
Consider some identities you have – parent, spouse, friend, worker, retiree. What most defines you? Pray for God's strength in the roles you have.

READ
Psalm 31

EXPLORE
This psalm records the anguish of a person under siege – physically (v 21) and emotionally (v 9). Strength is failing (v 10). It is not only enemies that are the problem. Even close friends are turning away (v 11). The psalmist is alone, surrounded by whispers and betrayal (v 13). How easy to be crushed at times such as this. So often we let circumstances or others' opinions define us.

Yet there is another way. Note the psalmist's defiant 'but' in verse 14. The psalmist looks to God to be his refuge and strength (vs 2,3). His life is in God's hands (v 15). When the world is falling apart, God alone can be trusted to set his people in a secure and 'spacious place' (v 8).

This prayer of lament by David has been used by believers throughout the centuries in times of distress and danger.

Jesus prayed it as he hung on the cross (Luke 23:46). Despite those who betrayed him he was confident of who he was and God's purposes for him. The psalm can help us do the same. We can discover our true identity as a child of God and, like Jesus, say, 'Into your hands I commit my spirit' (v 5).

> But I trust in you, Lord; I say, 'You are my God.'

Psalm 31:14

RESPOND
In this coming week watch out for times when difficulties or the opinions of others begin to shape your identity. Refuse to be shaped by this. Be who you really are.

Bible in a year: Exodus 11,12; Matthew 22

The perils of leadership

PREPARE

'Remember your leaders, who spoke the word of God to you' (Hebrews 13:7). Pray for these leaders today.

READ

Numbers 11:1–35

EXPLORE

Being a leader is no easy thing. We see this in Moses' response to the all-too-familiar complaints of the Israelites. How quickly these people have forgotten all that God has done. They are still looking back to Egypt with rose-coloured glasses (vs 4,5). Moses complains that 'these people' are like petulant children, never satisfied (vs 12,13). He feels alone and overwhelmed (v 15). Which of us with leadership responsibilities have not felt the same?

Moses' problem is that he fails to be objective. He thinks that God is displeased with *him* (v 11). In his despair he forgets that Israel's leadership was not his responsibility alone. As one writer observes, 'The trouble with depression is that it maximises the problems and minimises the resources.'* A lesson for us all. The Lord answers Moses' prayer. He empowers seventy elders with the spirit to share Moses' burden (vs 16,17).

Joshua's objection is overruled by Moses who wishes that *all* God's people be filled with the Spirit (vs 28,29). His wish is fulfilled at Pentecost as God's Spirit is poured out with abundance (Acts 2).

As for the people, they get what they demand, plus judgement (vs 31–34). Their craving for food leads to their graves in the desert. Not a great beginning for their journey.

> The LORD answered Moses, 'Is the LORD's arm too short? Now you will see whether or not what I say will come true for you.'
>
> **Numbers 11:23**

RESPOND

Whether you need help to do ministry, or food for the table, bring to God your needs.

*Raymond Brown, *The Message of Numbers*, Bible Speaks Today series, IVP, 2002, p94.

Bible in a year: Exodus 13,14; Matthew 23

Being colour-blind

PREPARE
Give thanks for the spread of the gospel throughout the world – people of every nation, tribe and tongue gathered up in God's new family.

READ
Numbers 12:1–16

EXPLORE
More rebellion within God's people, but for Moses this time it's closer to home. The passage contains issues that still cause grief and pain today – sibling rivalry, leadership tensions and the issue of racism. Moses' wife was an outsider from Cush, modern-day Ethiopia.

The Lord chastises Aaron and Miriam for speaking against their brother. As important as their roles as priest and prophetess, Moses' task is unique – he is the one to whom God speaks direct (v 8). Criticising him is like criticising God himself. Miriam's judgement seems fitting. If skin colour is a problem, then let that be for her as well (v 10). If Moses' wife is to be socially excluded, then let Miriam experience exclusion herself (v 15).

This is a challenging passage. For the early Christians, the issue was incorporating the Gentiles into a predominantly Jewish church (Acts 15; Romans 9–11). God's kingdom was not about exclusion but the inclusion of all – even those who seem different and strange. As Paul declared, 'There is neither Jew nor Gentile, neither slave nor free, nor is there male and female, for you are all one in Christ Jesus' (Galatians 3:28). What does this mean for your own church community? Are there barriers to be broken?

> Miriam and Aaron began to talk against Moses because of his Cushite wife, for he had married a Cushite.
>
> **Numbers 12:1**

RESPOND
Consider those you spend time with at your church. Are they mostly like you? In what ways can you reach out to the 'different' ones around you?

Scripture Union

By purchasing *Daily Bread*, you are helping to support Scripture Union's mission with children and young people. Thank you!

Subscribe to our free supporter and prayer magazine at su.org.uk/ connectingyou

So close, yet so far

God's people were so close. In a few months they had been rescued from slavery in Egypt through the Red Sea, led through the wilderness by a cloud and fiery pillar, and been fed by miraculous manna and quail. Now, here they stand at the border of the land promised to their forefathers. It's like a film that feels as if it's about to end, but you have an hour left. 'What on earth is there left to happen?' you ask yourself.

God's people were so close, yet so far: they were a 'rabble' (11:4); Moses' own siblings had opposed him (chapter 12); and now in chapters 13–19 their rebellion goes from bad to worse, resulting in thousands being killed and the rest being condemned to wandering in the wilderness for forty years. It doesn't make sense that people who had witnessed such wonders would rebel within months and wish they were back in Egypt – as slaves (14:3,4)! The Israelites had been set free, but didn't want to change. They had seen, but did not trust. They had heard, but did not listen.

Looking back at all this Paul wrote: 'These things happened to them as examples and were written down as warnings for us … So, if you think you are standing firm, be careful that you don't fall!' (1 Corinthians 10:11,12). May we listen to and heed these warnings, and make sure we are standing on the only firm ground of God's forgiveness in Jesus.

About the writer
Ben Green

Ben is married to Jess and they live in Selly Park, Birmingham, where he is a vicar and she is a doctor. When he isn't vicaring, Ben is most likely to be found either mowing his lawn or writing computer software, but he also enjoys walking up (real) mountains, playing the piano and letting Jess plan their holidays.

Giants and grasshoppers

PREPARE

The Israelite spies saw themselves as grasshoppers: small, weak, insignificant. How do you see yourself? How do you think God sees you? Close your eyes and ask God to help you see yourself as he does.

· ·

READ

Numbers 13:1–3,17–33

EXPLORE

The spies' journey through Canaan ended in Hebron (v 22), where Abraham had purchased a cave as the family tomb: he was buried there, alongside Sarah, Isaac and Jacob. The purchase of a tomb in a foreign land was a sign of Abraham's faith in God's promise, repeated here to his descendants (v 1). The spies' visit, after all these centuries, was a sign of God's faithfulness to that promise.

It looked good: the tomb, the cluster of grapes so big they named the area 'Cluster Valley' (v 24), the flowing milk and honey (v 27). Yet the spies began their report with an accusation ('the land to which *you sent us*') not an expression of faith (the land God is *giving us*, v 2). And it went from bad to worse: the spies showed no faith, even as God was proving himself faithful.

Despite the best efforts of Caleb (v 30) and Joshua (14:6–9), the bad report spread (v 32). The people focused on themselves – 'we seemed like grasshoppers' (v 33) – instead of God, who was faithfully fulfilling his promises.

> 'We seemed like grasshoppers in our own eyes, and we looked the same to them.'
>
> **Numbers 13:33**

RESPOND

Faith means trusting that God is bigger than our problems. The spies held their faith-binoculars the wrong way round: magnifying their problem and minimising their God. Ask God to help you hold your faith-binoculars the right way round.

· ·

Bible in a year: Exodus 17,18; Matthew 24

Thursday 3 February
Numbers 14:1–25

Rebels without reason

PREPARE

Do you like a good grumble? Do you enjoy a whinge and a moan? When you're part of a group that starts being negative, are you a spreader or a stopper?

READ

Numbers 14:1–25

EXPLORE

The rabble made a proper racket, lifting up their voices, crying, weeping (v 1). The faithless spies had set the whole community on fire with their faithless words; see how many times the words 'all', 'whole', 'entire' appear in verses 1–10.

Against all reason the people rejected God and questioned his power, his promise, and his plan – with some passion! They threatened faithful Caleb and Joshua with the punishment they themselves deserved (v 10); it was only Moses' prayers that saved them (vs 13–19).

What do you make of verses 20–23? How can God both forgive (v 20) and punish his people (vs 21–23)? First, the people totally rejected God (v 4), so deserved total punishment (v 12). God showed mercy by caring for them all in the wilderness (see Nehemiah 9:16–21), and giving their children the Promised Land. Second, forgiveness is never free. Under the Law, forgiveness came through costly sacrifice; the forgiveness was and is real, but the price had to be paid. Thank God Jesus has paid that price for us!

> All the Israelites grumbled against Moses and Aaron ... 'If only we had died in Egypt!'
>
> **Numbers 14:2**

RESPOND

Moses interceded on behalf of the people, and God forgave them – read verse 19 again. Intercession is hard work, and often a long journey. For whom is God calling you to intercede? How can you keep going and not give up?

Bible in a year: Exodus 19,20; Matthew 25

Pride and punishment

PREPARE

It isn't easy to read Bible passages about God's judgement. Spend a few moments focusing on the cross of Christ, and give thanks that Jesus died in our place, taking the punishment we deserve.

• •

READ

Numbers 14:26–45

EXPLORE

I was in my car, whining because I was stuck in a queue, late for a meeting, and in a foul mood. I honked my horn, twice. Imagine my horror when I turned the corner and saw the reason for the queue: a hearse bringing a coffin to church for a funeral!

The consequence of those angry honks hit me immediately, like the faithless spies' punishment (v 37). But sometimes the consequences of our actions take time to be worked out, like the people's punishment of forty years' wandering in the wilderness (v 34).

The people 'mourned bitterly' that night (v 39), but had learned the wrong lesson; it wasn't 'you can win', but '*listen* to the Lord your God'. Moses begged them not to go (v 41) – why? Because the people of the land *were* too strong for the Israelites (see 13:31) so they would lose

without God fighting for them – and so they did (v 44,45). To listen to God *and do what he says* is a hard lesson to learn for proud people. That doesn't include us though, does it?

> So tell them, 'As surely as I live, declares the LORD, I will do to you the very thing I heard you say...'
>
> **Numbers 14:28**

RESPOND

Hebrews encourages us to heed the warning of the rebellion of these people (Hebrews 3,4). Ask God to help you see if and how you have been ignoring something he's been telling you to do or to stop.

• •

Bible in a year: Exodus 21,22; Psalm 17

Saturday 5 February
Numbers 15:22–41

The seriousness of sin

PREPARE
Of all the sin in your life, which is the area or one thing where you are most stubborn and refuse to stop? Maybe you've been warned or had opportunities to ask for help and ignored them?

READ
Numbers 15:22–41

EXPLORE
How seriously do we really take sin? Do you agree that sometimes we focus too much on God's forgiveness and minimise his command to live a holy life?

Here God teaches us about sin through two contrasts. The first is between community sin (vs 22–26) and individual sin (vs 27–29). We are perhaps more used to the latter – how about the former? It includes things like systemic racism, injustice, unconscious bias: they are hard to spot unless we experience them. Do you resist them, or perpetuate them (unwittingly or otherwise)? The second is between accidental sin (vs 22–29) and defiant sin (vs 30,31), part of which must be an unrepentant attitude. What do you think 'despising' the Lord's word (v 31) might mean?

It is reassuring that God has realistic expectations! He knows our weakness, and graciously provides a way of forgiveness without minimising the seriousness of sin. Read verse 28 again – for us 'the priest' is Jesus – and rejoice in how that verse ends.

> 'Remember to obey all my commands.'
> **Numbers 15:40**

RESPOND
What might be the equivalent of the Israelites' tassels (vs 38,39) for you? What could you do, or wear, or have on the wall to remind you of God's command and call to live a holy life?

Bible in a year: Exodus 23,24; Matthew 26

The cover up

PREPARE

If you are in the Northern Hemisphere, there is every chance it might be snowing right now. Even if not, close your eyes and picture the way snow covers everything as it falls so silently and so beautifully.

READ

Psalm 32

EXPLORE

I like a good pun... did you hear about the man who was fired from the calendar factory? All he did was take a day off! David was in punning mood when he penned this psalm: he uses the same word for 'covered' (v 1 – like snow covers the ground) and 'cover up' (v 5 – like politicians cover up a scandal).

Whatever his sin was – traditionally, but not necessarily, his adultery with Bathsheba – he tried to hide it at first (v 3), claiming 'to be without sin' (1 John 1:8). That didn't go well. What do you think it means that God's hand was 'heavy' on David (v 4)? Is that something you recognise?

Eventually he admitted what he had done; he stopped covering it up himself (v 5) and let God cover it for him (v 1). Compare verses 4 and 11. What a difference being honest and confessing

his sin made to David! Are you brave enough to learn his lesson (v 8)?

> Blessed is the one whose transgressions are forgiven, whose sins are covered.
>
> **Psalm 32:1**

RESPOND

The Bible tells us that God does not change. What he did for David, he can and will do for you. Spend some time confessing your sin, using words inspired by this psalm. Ask God to help you know the joy of verse 11.

Bible in a year: Exodus 25,26; Matthew 27

Monday 7 February
Numbers 16:1–7,31–35,46–50

Crossing the line

PREPARE

Do you know the feeling when you take something too far? When you cross the line? Do you ever feel that way about complaints in your church family about your church leader(s)?

READ

Numbers 16:1–7,31–35,46–50

EXPLORE

Like a leaking sewer, the stench of sin spreads far and wide. The pride of a handful (v 1) spread to 250 more (v 2) and then the 'whole community' (v 41). This happened 3,500 years ago but people don't change: how have you seen this play out in your circles, even in your church?

Korah and the others were thinking on a human level. He was a Levite, and they had special responsibilities (v 9) but they weren't *in charge*. In fact, neither were priests – God was, and is – but Korah was fixated on human status and power. He compared himself to Aaron instead of focusing on being faithful to his own role serving God's people. That is what God cares about: the role doesn't matter, our faithfulness to his call does.

In his pride, Korah crossed the line and took others with him. The consequences were serious and terrifying (vs 31–34). Yet Aaron saved many, standing between the living and the dead (vs 47,48): exactly as our priest Jesus does for us when *our* pride makes *us* cross the line.

'You have gone too far!'

Numbers 16:3,7

RESPOND

Pray for those who lead you in your church family, in whatever sense – be imaginative in seeing how different people lead you! Then ask God to help you listen and be faithful as the person he's called you to be.

Bible in a year: Exodus 27,28; Matthew 28

Elected leadership

PREPARE

What do you do when you reach the end of your tether? Personally, I tend to rant and rave and collapse in a heap! How do you show it when you have really had enough?

READ

Numbers 17:1–13

EXPLORE

We don't know the timescale of these chapters – days, months, years – but we know the grumbling was constant (v 5). I imagine Moses had had enough: the people were too busy grumbling to *listen*. Yesterday we saw God respond to the grumbling with signs of judgement; today he offers a sign of election, not by democratic vote, but by divine appointment (v 5).

But why almonds (v 8)? Whether or not you like marzipan, it seems an odd detail but it's a powerful image. Almond blossom is white, pure as snow; also, almonds were expensive and highly prized. When sending his sons to Pharaoh, Jacob counted them among the 'best products of the land' (Genesis 43:11). Then, in Hebrew, 'almond tree' sounds like 'watching' (Jeremiah 1:11,12).

The almond-budded staff was therefore a sign of the person God chose *and* their role: to be an example of purity and holiness, to be valued, to keep watch over God's people. Sadly, it was a sign God's people needed then, and in perpetuity (v 10).

> 'The staff belonging to the man I choose will sprout...'
> **Numbers 17:5**

RESPOND

The priestly mediator role, standing between us and God, is fulfilled by Jesus. But there is still a place for leadership and authority within the church. Ask God to show you how you can affirm and encourage those who lead you in your faith.

Bible in a year: Exodus 29,30; Psalm 18

Giving generously

PREPARE
How do you decide what you spend your money on? How we spend reveals our priorities – where does giving to the church fit into that? Is it 'one charity among many', or something more?

READ
Numbers 18:1–32

EXPLORE
Remember Korah? He got stuck on the all-too-human concerns of status and power. He forgot three important principles of leadership in God's family: it is limited (v 3), it is a gift not a right (v 7), and it is an act of service (v 7). Is that how you see leadership within the church? Or are you closer to Korah's attitude, seeing leadership as something prestigious, to be grasped at?

Read verse 8 again. To whom were the Israelites' tithes given (also in vs 9,12–15,19)? Seven times it repeats: the tithes and sacrifices were given to *God*. He then offered them to the priests and Levites as a gift (eg v 11); this was a 'covenant of salt' (v 19) – solid, firm, unbreakable.

Without any inheritance (v 20) the priests needed the tithes to survive. That means tithing is at once both practical *and* spiritual: for God's people, giving is first an act of spiritual sacrifice, and second a practical way of supporting and enabling those who serve God's family.

'Whatever is set aside from the holy offerings ... is an everlasting covenant of salt before the LORD.'

Numbers 18:19

RESPOND
Giving is first to God (even if the church collects the cash and uses it to pay its bills!). Does that change how you see your money? Giving is more than money – but includes it. How generous are you? How generous could you be?

Bible in a year: Exodus 31,32; Acts 1

Dealing with dying

PREPARE

As a boy my favourite part of football was slide tackling... the muddier, the better! As we journey through life we collect 'mud' from sin, pain, death, struggle – how much do you need a 'wash'?

READ

Numbers 19:1–22

EXPLORE

Be honest: does this passage feel alien? It should, because we are dealing with a 3,500-year-old culture! But it's worth persevering.

For starters there is the simple reality of disease: washing after encountering a dead body in a world without antibiotics is sensible. More importantly, did you notice the heifer was to be sacrificed *whole*, including the blood (v 5)? Normally the blood of a sacrifice was poured out (eg Exodus 29:12, Leviticus 4:7). But here the blood, the *life* of the heifer, was left in and burned to ashes. As a result, the water of cleansing made with that ash (v 17) contained a powerful sign of life. So, if the uncleanness of death is made clean by that which sustains life, what does that tell us about life and death? Which is more powerful?

We may be tempted to cope with the pain of death by minimising it as 'nothing at all' or being 'in the next room'. But this ancient ritual teaches us a truth of real comfort: although death is real, life is stronger.

> 'They must purify themselves with the water on the third day ... then they will be clean.'
>
> **Numbers 19:12**

RESPOND

More powerful than the water of cleansing is the blood of Jesus, which washes us from all uncleanness *and* rescues us from death. All that 'mud' you thought about earlier – ask Jesus to clean you inside and out, and give you his new life.

Bible in a year: Exodus 33,34; Acts 2

The Jesus letters

I still get excited whenever I receive a handwritten letter through the post. There is something special about a personal communication like this, quite different from an email or text message.

When the apostle John was imprisoned on the Greek island of Patmos, he received a revelation from God about the events that would soon take place. He was told to write down what he saw and send the content to the seven churches in Asia Minor. There was a specific message from Jesus for each church, so it was like seven letters in one. Imagine the excitement of the leaders in these churches as they read what Jesus had to say to them!

While each message is distinct, the format of the letters is quite similar:

An introduction – who is speaking?

An encouragement – what is going well?

A challenge – what could be better?

Some advice – how can we improve?

In these readings, we will focus simply on the word of encouragement that is given by Jesus to each church. We can learn from this what Jesus looks for in his church, and this can be a stimulus to help us evaluate how we are doing in our own churches.

About the writer
Tony Horsfall

After graduating from London School of Theology, Tony served as a missionary in East Malaysia, then as a pastor in West Yorkshire. Since 2004 he has had his own ministry, Charis Training. He is a retreat leader, author and mentor.

Jesus loves the church

PREPARE

Ask God to speak to you as we begin these readings in Revelation, in particular about the church of which you are a part, and that he loves, despite its shortcomings.

READ

Revelation 1:1–8

EXPLORE

Churches vary considerably in their beliefs, worship style and ministry philosophy but they have one thing in common – they belong to Jesus. This doxology describes three aspects of what he has done for us.

He loves us (v 5b). This simple truth is at the heart of everything, the foundation stone on which our faith rests. Love brought him into the world, took Jesus to the cross, and love flows from his heart and his throne in heaven.

He has freed us (v 5b). His death was the sacrifice that made atonement for our sins. He died in our place, giving his life as a ransom to set us free from sin's penalty and power. We have been redeemed, and the liberating power of the cross is still at work in us today.

He has made us (v 6). The purpose of God is being worked out in the world through the church. We are called to be the expression of his kingdom, living under his rule and reign, and demonstrating his goodness to a watching world. At the same time, we are called to be worshippers, standing before him as priests and declaring his praises.

> To him who loves us and has freed us from our sins by his blood, and has made us to be a kingdom and priests to serve his God and Father – to him be glory and power...

Revelation 1:5,6

RESPOND

Do you know you are loved by Jesus? Are you allowing him to set you free from anything unhelpful in your life? Are you joining in his purpose for the church?

Bible in a year: Exodus 35,36; Psalm 19

Saturday 12 February
Revelation 1:9–20

Lord of the church

PREPARE
It's the weekend. Take a moment to be quiet and still. Relax yourself. Know again that God is present.

READ
Revelation 1:9–20

EXPLORE
I wonder what fears crowd into your mind today. What is worrying you or causing you stress? For a church living in the midst of a hostile pagan world there are plenty of good reasons to be afraid. So, here is a reassuring reminder that Jesus, the Lord of the church, places his strong hand upon us to comfort and strengthen us.

He is Lord of history (v 17). Everything began with him (the First), and everything will end with him (the Last). And in between, all is well because his purpose is being worked out, despite the wiles of Satan and the persecution of the world.

He is Lord of life (v 18). At the cross he defeated death and now lives again to lead and guide his church. We are not alone. The Living One is with us.

He is Lord of the future (v 18). The keys are in his hands, meaning that all authority has been given to Jesus. The destiny of the world and individuals is with him.

We are invited to turn our eyes upon Jesus and see him in his glory (vs 12–16). Here is the antidote to fear and despair – knowing that Jesus is Lord.

'Do not be afraid. I am the First and the Last. I am the Living One; I was dead, and now look, I am alive for ever and ever!'
Revelation 1:17,18

RESPOND
Where is your gaze today? Take a moment to remind yourself that he is in control and you have nothing to fear. Hand your concerns over to him.

Bible in a year: Exodus 37,38; Acts 3

Reasons to be glad

PREPARE

John was in the Spirit on the Lord's Day (1:10). Allow the Holy Spirit to fill you afresh as you come to God's Word.

READ

Psalm 33

EXPLORE

Being grateful is one of the best ways to lift your spirit when the going is tough. Resilient people know that giving thanks in the midst of difficult circumstances lifts your spirit, gives glory to God, and enables you to keep going. Search this psalm for reasons to be glad today. Here are some ideas.

For the character of God – who is faithful in all he does (v 4). Consider the ways in which he has shown himself to be faithful to you.

For the word of the Lord – by which the heavens were made (v 6). Why not make time today to look up and see the beauty of the sky or stand outside when it is dark and see the universe that he brought into being?

For the reliability of the purposes of God (v 11). Even now, his plans are being worked out in the world, and his plans for your life will come to pass in his good time. Why not express your trust in him?

For the care that God has for us (vs 18,19), watching over us and providing for us. Thank him for his unfailing love. Remember times when God has clearly helped or protected you.

Sing joyfully to the LORD, you righteous; it is fitting for the upright to praise him.

Psalm 33:1

RESPOND

Make this prayer your own today, repeating it slowly several times: 'May your unfailing love rest upon me, O Lord, even as I put my trust in you' (based on v 22).

Bible in a year: Exodus 39,40; Acts 4

Monday 14 February
Revelation 2:1–7

Perseverance

PREPARE
What challenges are before you today as a new working week begins? Remind yourself that, even if you feel overwhelmed, God is there to help you carry the load.

READ
Revelation 2:1–7

EXPLORE

Perseverance is one of the great Bible words, and a key characteristic of Christian discipleship (v 3). It is the ability to keep going in the midst of difficulty and hardship, not quitting because life is hard but choosing, with God's help, to make it through to the end. 'Resilience' is a more modern word, with the connotation of bouncing back after setbacks or difficulties.

The church in Ephesus figures prominently in the New Testament, having been founded by the apostle Paul and then cared for by his young protégé, Timothy. One of the things that Jesus, as Lord of the church, appreciates about this congregation is their consistency – they have worked hard and not given up, despite being troubled by false apostles (v 2). They have endured hardship and not grown weary.

How is this possible? Only when we look to God for daily strength. This means taking time as you are doing today to be still in God's presence, in order to receive his strength through prayer and the Scriptures. Worship also plays its part, as does the encouragement of fellowship with other believers.

> 'You have persevered and have endured hardships for my name, and have not grown weary.'
>
> **Revelation 2:3**

RESPOND

As you look back on your life, can you remember times when God brought you through difficult times? Take encouragement from such memories, as you look to God now to help you through today's challenges.

Bible in a year: Leviticus 1–3; Acts 5

Faithfulness

PREPARE
Most of us suffer from distracting thoughts when we come to read and pray. Pause before you begin today and breathe slowly, asking God to help you focus.

READ
Revelation 2:8–11

EXPLORE

The verse below was given to me at my baptismal service, as an encouragement for the life of discipleship that lay ahead of me. That was over 50 years ago, and by the grace of God I am still following Jesus today, although it has not always been easy.

Faithfulness is another great Christian characteristic, which is often underrated. There is nothing spectacular about it, and the church in Smyrna itself seems to have been an unspectacular kind of church. But the ability to stick to a task, to see things through to the end, to keep going with a loyal and steadfast determination, is something commended by Jesus.

There is, however, another aspect of faithfulness that is far more costly, and that is the decision to remain true to Jesus in the face of opposition. The church in Smyrna is warned that they will soon be called upon to suffer for their faith (v 10). Indeed, the Spirit tells them that some will be thrown into prison for ten days. Satan will test their faith – will they remain true to Jesus? How might I fare under such a prospect? How courageous am I?

'Be faithful, even to the point of death, and I will give you life as your victor's crown.'
Revelation 2:10

RESPOND
Where do you need to be faithful? How do you face opposition to your faith – at work, from your family and friends, in the attitudes of society? Pray for believers for whom physical persecution is a daily reality.

Bible in a year: Leviticus 4,5; Psalms 20,21

Distinctiveness

PREPARE
Our access into God's presence does not depend on how we feel, or how well we have performed. Jesus has opened up for us a new and living way, and we can come boldly into his presence.

••

READ
Revelation 2:12–17

EXPLORE
One of the British TV programmes I enjoy is called *Escape to the Country*. It follows the story of people seeking to move from the bustle of the city to the peace and quiet of the country.

Not all of us can live in such idyllic locations. Pergamum was an idolatrous city, filled with pagan shrines, and with the temple of Zeus dominating the skyline. The believers who lived there experienced great opposition as well as spiritual oppression. It felt like it was the very headquarters of Satan and his demonic forces. One of the church members, Antipas, had even been martyred, yet the believers stood firm in their faith (v 13).

What an encouragement therefore to hear Jesus say, 'I know where you live...' (v 13). Jesus is present in even the darkest places and most undesirable neighbourhoods, watching over his people and strengthening their faith. And today you can be certain that he knows where you live – not just the geographical location, but the circumstances in which you live. He is aware of your challenges, the pressures upon you, and the temptations you face. He knows your situation and is there to help you.

'I know where you live – where Satan has his throne. Yet you remain true to my name.'
Revelation 2:13

RESPOND
Where do you live? How would you describe that place? What is the spiritual atmosphere like? Remember that Jesus is with you wherever you are.

••

Bible in a year: Leviticus 6,7; Acts 6

Service

PREPARE

Having 'ears to hear' means to be attentive to what God is saying. Pray that you will be sensitive to the voice of the Spirit as you read and pray today.

READ

Revelation 2:18–29

EXPLORE

No church is perfect and the church in Thyatira had allowed ungodly influences to seep into its very being. Even so, the believers there are commended for their lively service for God, which had not gone unnoticed.

Faith has to be put into practice, otherwise it is dead (James 2:14–17). Every local church is to consider how best to serve God in their community, reaching out with practical help and sensitive outreach. Such good deeds are not to earn us favour with God but to express our love and our faith. We serve others because the love of Christ constrains us, and we get involved in various projects because our faith prompts us to do so.

The activity level of the church in Thyatira was increasing, too, and they were doing more than previously (v 19). There is of course a danger here. We can be so busy doing things *for* God that we forget to be *with* God. Over-extending ourselves can lead to individual burnout and community weariness, but it need not be so if what we do is done in his strength and under his direction.

> '**I know your deeds, your love and faith, your service and perseverance, and that you are now doing more than you did at first.'**
>
> **Revelation 2:19**

RESPOND

What opportunity do you have to serve God in your church and community? Are you doing too little, or too much? Pray that what you do will be motivated by love and sustained by faith.

Bible in a year: Leviticus 8,9; Acts 7

Friday 18 February
Revelation 3:1–6

Revival!

PREPARE
Hunger for God is not a virtue we possess, but a gift from God. Left to ourselves we can all become complacent. Pray that God will stir your heart afresh today.

READ
Revelation 3:1–6

EXPLORE

Have you noticed how churches have a reputation of their own? One church has good Bible teaching, another is known for its fabulous worship, a third offers amazing youth ministry. There is a danger though that churches can live on their reputation or history, not realising that spiritually they have fallen asleep and lost their way.

Many people pray for revival in the nation, and that is good and commendable, but revival must begin first in the church. The church in Sardis had become comfortable, indeed so comfortable it had fallen asleep (vs 1–3). This spiritual slumber had caused them to become lax and careless. They needed to be woken up, to be revived before it was too late.

The antidote to complacency is repentance, to acknowledge that things are not as they should be, and to seek to put things right. Repentance and revival go hand in hand. Once we humble ourselves and admit our need, not only will God forgive us, but his reviving Spirit will flow into us again. What a difference it would make if our churches were throbbing again with divine life!

> 'Wake up! Strengthen what remains and is about to die, for I have found your deeds unfinished in the sight of my God.'
>
> **Revelation 3:2**

RESPOND
Pray that you personally will be revived, repenting if necessary. Pray that the church that you belong to will not rest on its laurels but experience renewal and revival.

Bible in a year: Leviticus 10–12; Psalm 22

Responsive

PREPARE
Perhaps today you feel you have little strength? Maybe the past week was difficult. Jesus knows your feelings, whether of weakness or inadequacy. Rest in his love.

READ
Revelation 3:7–13

EXPLORE
I visited Stormont castle in Belfast with a friend. After a long walk around the grounds, we returned to the main gates to find them firmly closed. They were too high to scale and I imagined being locked in all night. We backtracked and after another long walk found a tiny gate through which we could exit, somewhat exhausted.

Jesus is the one who opens and closes doors (v 7). If he opens a door, no one can close it; if he closes a door, no one can open it. In this context the door refers to a door of opportunity, for ministry and witness. God is placing before the church in Philadelphia a new opportunity to serve him.

Here is a major principle of guidance. Generally speaking, if a particular course of action or direction is God's will, then the door will open. If it is not, then the door will remain closed and no amount of pushing will make it open. This requires us to be sensitive and responsive to God's leading, to recognise when an opportunity is God-given. Likewise, to understand when God is closing a particular path to us and to accept that.

> 'See, I have placed before you an open door that no one can shut. I know that you have little strength, yet you have kept my word and have not denied my name.'
>
> **Revelation 3:8**

RESPOND
Consider any matter of guidance that concerns you. If you sense the door is open, will you take the opportunity? If it seems closed, can you accept that this is not the way for you?

Bible in a year: Leviticus 13,14; Acts 8

Sunday 20 February
Psalm 34

The nearness of God

PREPARE
In the midst of your busyness, let today be a different day, a day set apart for God, for rest and recreation. How will you do this?

READ
Psalm 34

EXPLORE
This psalm is of David. He had fled to the Philistine king, Abimelech, for refuge from Saul who was seeking his life. However, when the Philistines discovered who he was, David had to flee again for safety.

The psalm is full of rich insight into how to find strength from God in difficult days – notice the mention of such words as fears, troubles and afflictions. It is all about seeing God as our refuge (vs 8,22) and crying out to him for help (vs 4,6,17) in the assurance that God will come to our aid (v 22).

The nearness of God in times of trouble is highlighted for us. The broken-hearted are those who have suffered loss, disappointment and grief in their relationships. Their emotions are shattered and the pain is excruciating. The crushed in spirit are those who have been overwhelmed by the demands of life and are weary and exhausted, full of despair and with no hope (v 18).

At such times, God draws near to us, to bind up our wounds and lift our burdens. God may feel a million miles away but in fact he is right there with us sharing our pain.

The LORD is close to the broken-hearted and saves those who are crushed in spirit.
Psalm 34:18

RESPOND
David's response to difficulty is to praise God regardless (v 1). No matter how you feel today, take time to lift up your voice in praise.

Bible in a year: Leviticus 15,16; Acts 9

Honesty

PREPARE

Today's reading reminds us that Jesus stands at the door and knocks, seeking to gain admission into our lives (v 20). Will you let him in?

· ·

READ
Revelation 3:14–22

EXPLORE

Self-awareness and self-knowledge are crucial ingredients in spiritual growth, enabling transformation into the likeness of Christ. Without this willingness to be radically honest with ourselves, we will always be in danger of self-deceit, thinking we are better than we really are.

The church in Laodicea is remembered because of its lukewarmness, but that complacency was the result of a lack of understanding of their true condition (v 17). It was a prosperous and successful place, and the church there was a smart and wealthy one, but without any sense of need. Instead, it prided itself on being self-sufficient.

Out of his love, Jesus says he will discipline the church, probably by allowing the fires of adversity to purify them of their pride and reveal to them their deep need of him (v 19). Self-knowledge often only comes through suffering and trial. It is when we are broken that we can best see our need of Jesus (v 20).

Afflictions serve a purpose in our lives, that of humbling us and making us aware of our true condition. Fortunately, the grace of God is such that he welcomes us as we are and builds us up again.

> 'You say, "I am rich; I have acquired wealth and do not need a thing." But you do not realise that you are wretched, pitiful, poor, blind and naked.'
> **Revelation 3:17**

RESPOND

How are you growing in your understanding of yourself, both strengths and weaknesses? How honest are you prepared to be? How is God teaching you to be more dependent on him?

Bible in a year: Leviticus 17,18; Acts 10

Scripture Union

A legacy of love

Could you leave a gift in your will and ensure the good news of Jesus is shared with generations to come?

TO FIND OUT MORE, VISIT SU.ORG.UK/LEGACY OR CALL 01908 856120

'...we will tell the next generation the praiseworthy deeds of the Lord, his power, and the wonders he has done.' **Psalm 78:4**

The painful road to glory

About the writer
David Lawrence

David is the Teaching Pastor at Thornbury Baptist Church, near Bristol. He is married with three children and six grandchildren. Alongside his ministry at Thornbury, he runs a gardening and woodworking business.

The book of 'Revelation' is Jesus' message (1:1) to his puzzled and persecuted followers.

As we've seen in chapters 1–3, its first readers were situated in local churches across modern Turkey. They were experiencing increasing hostility from the Roman authorities, making life hard for all of them and causing some to even lose their lives (2:13). Experiencing hardship and suffering must have left them puzzled. 'How can God be in charge if things are so bleak?' Perhaps we sometimes ask that question too. If so, these chapters begin to supply an answer.

Significantly, the first thing we see in heaven is God on his throne (4:2) surrounded by worshippers (4:6–11). Whatever chaos may follow, God's sovereignty is history's anchor. A scroll is seen in God's hand (5:1), symbolising the unfolding of world history and Jesus (the Lamb who had been slain: 5:6) is given the responsibility of opening the scroll. As he does so, we see in the subsequent chapters how the unfolding, chaotic story of life on earth is shaped by events in the spirit-world of the heavens.

Using its bizarre imagery, coded number systems, sophisticated structure, and frequent Old Testament references, the rest of Revelation carries a simple but vital message: God is on heaven's throne and, despite the evil that is all around, King Jesus reigns: so, keep the faith, and don't lose your eternal reward in God's renewed creation! (2:7; 3:5; 4:4; 21:1–5; 22:12,13)

Tuesday 22 February
Revelation 4:1–11

Look up

PREPARE
'I look up to the mountains – does my help come from there? My help comes from the Lord, who made heaven and earth!' (Psalm 121:1,2, NLT). What do you need help for today? Talk to God about it.

READ
Revelation 4:1–11

EXPLORE
What a privilege! We are invited to accompany John, through the thin veil separating earth and heaven (v 1) and we immediately find ourselves in the epicentre of creation – God's throne room (v 2). In our journey into the subsequent chapters, we must never lose the golden thread tying us to this moment and this great truth: God is on the throne of history.

This whole chapter is designed to cement God's sovereignty into our consciousness. Shouts of praise constantly echo around the throne room (vs 8,11) as all of creation (symbolised by the four fantastic creatures in verses 6 and 7) and all his people (the 24 elders are symbolic figureheads of God's people in every age – 12 Old Testament patriarchs and 12 apostles) worship him.

One can only imagine the effect this vision must have had on the embattled Christians who first heard it read in the context of their hardships and suffering. Despite all appearances, when they paused to look up, God was still supreme.

What effect does this vision have on you, in your context today?

> At once I was in the Spirit, and there before me was a throne in heaven with someone sitting on it.
>
> **Revelation 4:2**

RESPOND
Bring to mind the events of your day. Hold them as you prayerfully reflect on these words from the hymn: 'Be Thou my vision ... /... whatever befall, / Still be my vision, O Ruler of all.' (Traditional. English version, Eleanor Hull, 1912.)

Bible in a year: Leviticus 19,20; Psalms 23,24

The heart of worship

PREPARE

Stop. Stop planning, worrying, rushing and, especially, stop taking control. Be still. Think about one thing: you are in the presence of the Living God, of perfect Love, endless grace and mercy. Stop. Receive his presence. Know yourself accepted.

READ

Revelation 5:1–14

EXPLORE

The thunder of heaven's worshippers in the three hymns in this chapter (9,10,12,13,14) must have been spine-tingling! Their songs (v 9) and shouts (v 12) were all focused on a Lamb, that had signs of having died but was now very much alive (vs 6,8,12). The Lamb signifies Jesus, crucified and now resurrected, receiving heaven's adulation with, and as, God himself (v 13). But what has caused such a cascade of praise?

Jesus has overcome a grave problem. No one could be found who was good enough to open and bring into effect God's plans for salvation (the scroll of verses 1–3). With God's purposes sealed up, history is in the control of darkness: the suffering Christians and the world itself have no hope. Enter the Lamb (v 5): the powerful, all-seeing, Spirit-guided (v 6) King Jesus! The cosmos has hope, in the shape of a suffering, resurrected King.

How do you keep your vision of Jesus fresh, such that it inspires you to praise? Meditating on the songs in this chapter is guaranteed to take you back to the heart of worship.

In a loud voice they were saying: 'Worthy is the Lamb, who was slain, to receive power and wealth and wisdom and strength and honour and glory and praise!'

Revelation 5:12

RESPOND

What is your favourite Jesus-focused hymn or worship song? Find the words or a recording and use it now to join heaven's celebration and worship the Lamb on the throne!

Bible in a year: Leviticus 21,22; Acts 11

Thursday 24 February
Revelation 6:1–17

How long?

PREPARE

'For waters shall break forth in the wilderness' (Isaiah 35:6, ESV). Your history does not define your destiny. God is the God of resurrection, the unexpected, and unearned, new life. Lay your 'wilderness' before God as you meditate on these words.

READ
Revelation 6:1–17

EXPLORE

As the scroll of history is opened, scenes of terror emerge. Led by a demonic 'false Messiah' (v 2), we see warfare (v 4), famine (v 6), cruel deaths (v 8) and cosmic upheaval (vs 12–14), and the presence of the One who sits on the throne strikes terror into the world's leaders (15–17).

But did you notice, the fifth seal reveals something different? Here we see God's people, martyred for their faith (v 9), now alive with him in heaven, crying out for justice (v 10). In the middle of turmoil in the world, God has them safe. Their death was not their end but, like the Lamb whom they followed, they lived on though 'slain'. Today, Christians around the world are being martyred for their faith, and all Christians live in a world all too similar to that described in this passage. This ancient vision describes a very contemporary world. How do we respond?

At the very least, like the souls under heaven's altar, we pray, loudly crying out to God for justice, and for God's final judgement (v 17) to unseat the riders of the four horses and put an end to all causes of suffering, pain, greed and evil.

> They called out in a loud voice, 'How long, Sovereign Lord, holy and true, until you judge the inhabitants of the earth and avenge our blood?'
>
> **Revelation 6:10**

RESPOND

There are many organisations working to support persecuted Christians. Pray for their work. Maybe visit their websites for up-to-date prayer requests, and to see how you can get involved.

Bible in a year: Leviticus 23,24; Acts 12

Help from heaven

PREPARE
Refresh your view of God as you mull and pray over this verse. 'O Lord, you are so good, so ready to forgive, so full of unfailing love for all who ask for your help' (Psalm 86:5, NLT).

READ
Revelation 7:1–17

EXPLORE
Today's reading is still in the sequence of the seven seals, that started in chapter 6, verse 1 and ends at chapter 8, verse 1. Destruction has been unleashed on the earth, in the form of the four horsemen (6:3–8). How can Christians keep their faith in such a world? Have you ever asked that question?

Today, we see that the answer comes in the form of supernatural help from heaven (v 1). To be sure, Christians will experience the woes that visit the earth, but it will not rob them of their most precious resource – their faith. God has sealed them (v 2) such that their faith can overcome the pressures that they experience (v 14). Miraculously, the same trials that harden the ungodly in their response to God (9:20,21) only serve to drive the faithful deeper into God's care (2:11,13).

But there is more. Christians live in hope: a fixed belief that God is in charge and will bring justice in the end. The beautiful heavenly rewards for the 'multitude' (v 9) of faithful believers are described in verses 15–17. They are motivation in themselves to 'keep the faith'!

'Do not harm the land or the sea or the trees until we put a seal on the foreheads of the servants of our God.'
Revelation 7:3

RESPOND
Pray for anyone you know personally whose faith is wilting under pressure. Pray for God's supernatural assistance.

Bible in a year: Leviticus 25,26; Psalm 25

God's prayer store

PREPARE

John Wesley often started his prayers by giving thanks for all God's blessings, 'spiritual and temporal'. What 'spiritual and temporal' blessings can you give thanks for today? Turn your thoughts into prayer.

READ

Revelation 8:1–13

EXPLORE

As history's final seal is opened (v 1), judgement ends – wars cease, suffering ends and the earth is still and silent before God (see Psalm 46:8–10). Finally, the prayers of the suffering saints (6:9,10) are answered, as God sends their stored intercessions hurtling to have their effect on the earth (3–5).

If you have ever wondered whether there was any point in praying; whether prayer actually changes anything at all, this image is a great encouragement to persevere. No prayer is wasted, even if currently it is waiting God's time.

As God answers the prayers of the saints for justice, we hear the first four of seven trumpets announcing God's war against all that is set against him in his world. Much of the imagery here echoes the plagues of the Exodus. God's warfare against all that oppresses his people was not just an historic act in Egypt, but a continuing one, and one which will climax as the seventh trumpet blows (but we must wait until chapter 11 for that!). In the meantime (spoiler alert): take heart, God wins.

> Another angel, who had a golden censer, came and stood at the altar. He was given much incense to offer, with the prayers of all God's people...
>
> **Revelation 8:3**

RESPOND

Are there any long-term prayers that remain unanswered for you? Find the courage to pray again, and put another deposit in God's prayer store.

Bible in a year: Leviticus 27; Numbers 1; Acts 13

Real prayer

PREPARE
Thank God for close friends and family who have stood by you in hard times. Ask God to bless them richly in this new week.

....

READ
Psalm 35

EXPLORE
Have you ever experienced a personal relationship gone sour? The psalmist knows what it feels like. People he formerly treated as friends (v 14) have turned against him. Instead of friendship there is now personal attack (v 1), threat (vs 4–8), unjust treatment (vs 11–16) and, even ridicule (vs 19–21).

It's easy to understand how painful this is, but even worse is that God appears to be indifferent (v 17). The psalmist has no doubt that God *could* do something about the pain that he is in (v 10), but right now that is not his experience. Have you ever been in that place?

The psalmist does the only thing he can: he prays. He protests about the injustice. He pours out his pain. He holds nothing back, but passionately, honestly and at length tells it like it is. This is no theological treatise on how to pray for your enemies (Matthew 5:43–45), but a raw outpouring of frustration.

It's OK to pray like that. God can handle it. In fact, maybe it's not until we pray like this that we are really praying at all.

> How long, Lord, will you look on? Rescue me from their ravages, my precious life from these lions.

Psalm 35:17

RESPOND
'And when you stand praying, if you hold anything against anyone, forgive them, so that your Father in heaven may forgive you your sins' (Mark 11:25). Is there anyone who has wronged you, that you need to forgive today? How will you communicate that forgiveness?

....

Bible in a year: Numbers 2,3; Acts 14

Monday 28 February
Revelation 9:1–21

Judgement and mercy

PREPARE
'He will wipe every tear from their eyes. There will be no more death or mourning or crying or pain...' (Revelation 21:4). Thank God for Christian hope.

READ
Revelation 9:1–21

EXPLORE
How do you react, as the seven trumpets of judgement continue to sound, intensifying in their severity (8:13)?

The fifth and sixth trumpets unleash demonic hordes, pictured as a plague of locusts (v 3), led by fallen satanic overseers (vs 1,11) bent on destruction. The sixth trumpet releases a great army (v 16), adding their dark power to the agonies on earth (v 18). It is hard to sugar-coat this picture of judgement, but three glimmers of light shine through the darkness.

In God's mercy, these acts are limited in duration and effect (vs 5,10,15,18).

Secondly, these are not random acts of violence, but 'earned' judgements by those who have rejected God and his ways (20b,21), and brutally oppressed God's people (6:9–11).

Thirdly, despite (or maybe because of) the horror, there is still the opportunity of repentance (v 20). These trumpet judgements are heavily based on the plagues against Pharaoh (Exodus 7–11) and, just as some of the ancient Egyptians escaped the plagues and joined God's people (Exodus 12:38), so, too, in God's grace, repentance is always a possibility, even in the worst of times.

> The rest of mankind who were not killed by these plagues still did not repent of the work of their hands.
>
> **Revelation 9:20a**

RESPOND
Pray this blessing for friends and family: 'May Christ Jesus guard and deliver you from the snares of the devil, from the assaults of evil spirits, from the wrath of the wicked, from all base passions, and from the fear of the known and unknown.'*

*Common Worship, Church of England.

Bible in a year: Numbers 4,5; Acts 15

Bitter-sweet faith

PREPARE

'Blessed be Your name / When the sun's shining down on me / When the world's 'all as it should be' / Blessed be Your name.'* Give thanks for the 'sunshine' in your life.

READ
Revelation 10:1–11

EXPLORE

If your experience of being a Christian were a weather condition, would it be sunny and calm, or wild, wet and windy?

Before the seventh trumpet heralds God's final judgement, we are offered an interlude (10:1 – 11:14). In today's vision, an angel appears holding a small scroll (v 2). The angel's stance on 'sea and land' (vs 2,5,8) suggests that its message has universal implications: God's cosmic plans are still on track (vs 6,7). His mysterious way of bringing ultimate victory through the suffering and apparent defeat of his people, will accomplish what he purposes (v 7).

The good news, however, is bittersweet (vs 9–11). It is impossible to separate Christian discipleship from suffering for Christ. Jesus never shied away from presenting both aspects of the good news to his would-be disciples, but counsels that bitter persecution and sweet joy need not be incompatible (Matthew 5:10–12)!

Periods of wild, wet and windy are part of the forecast but, despite the costs, this good news must be announced (v 11): there is no other salvation-story than that written on God's scroll!

> I took the little scroll from the angel's hand and ate it. It tasted as sweet as honey in my mouth, but when I had eaten it, my stomach turned sour.
>
> **Revelation 10:10**

RESPOND

'Blessed be Your name / On the road marked with suffering / Though there's pain in the offering / Blessed be Your name.'* Pray for any you know who are walking the road marked with suffering.

*From 'Blessed be your Name', Matt and Beth Redman, 2002.

Bible in a year: Numbers 6,7; Psalms 26,27

Wednesday 2 March
Revelation 11:1–19

Let your kingdom come

PREPARE
When you pray 'your kingdom come, your will be done, on earth as it is in heaven' (Matthew 6:10), what do you expect to happen as a result?

READ
Revelation 11:1–19

EXPLORE
I'm sure you have prayed 'your kingdom come' many times. In today's reading, we see that prayer, faithfully repeated by Christians throughout history, finally answered. God's kingdom comes (v 15) and his will alone is done on this earth, as it is in heaven (v 16).

That goal of history should inspire us through the dark days of 'this present age'. In language and imagery, again drawn from the Old Testament, the first part of our reading describes the faithful witness of the church (vs 3–6) through a period of opposition and even apparent defeat (vs 7–10): apparent, for we serve a God who raises the dead (vs 11,12)!

It is so easy to lose heart, to believe that we Christians form a small, insignificant minority, and even sometimes perhaps, to wonder if God is still in charge at all. This final reading in our series should encourage us that, even though we might indeed be a small minority, we are not insignificant, for our witness to the truth and our faithfulness to our Lord will one day be vindicated (v 18).

'The kingdom of the world has become the kingdom of our Lord and of his Messiah, and he will reign for ever and ever.'

Revelation 11:15

RESPOND
Christians are to live today, in the here-and-now, as citizens of God's coming kingdom. Our lives are to be a signpost and foretaste of a different world, where Jesus is fully in charge. What difference will that make to those around you today?

Bible in a year: Numbers 8,9; Acts 16

Finding hope in suffering

Job can be a difficult book to study, especially if you already know how it begins and ends. Little is known about its date and author.

In case you aren't familiar with the book, it opens with a conversation between God and Satan in which God asks Satan, 'Have you seen Job? Now there's a man who loves and serves me really well' (1:8). Satan replies, 'Of course he serves you; you only ever give him good things! If life wasn't so good for him, he would soon show his true colours' (1:9–11). So God allows Satan to strip away everything from Job to prove that his worship is much more than skin deep.

Knowing the reason for Job's afflictions gives us a very different perspective on them. In fact, much of the book is Job wrestling with the big 'Why?', and his so-called comforters trying to come up with answers. They try to diagnose the problem and help Job find the solution, but their diagnoses are way off the mark, and the book ends with God making them apologise.

So, is there anything we can learn from all the 'wrestling' chapters? The Bible teaches that 'All Scripture is God-breathed and is useful for teaching, rebuking, correcting and training in righteousness' (2 Timothy 3:16). So, Job chapters 22–31 must be there for a useful purpose. In the next few days, we will uncover together some hope-filled truths, as we consider how to think biblically about God, justice, righteousness and suffering.

About the writer
Jennie Pollock

Jennie is Head of Public Policy at the Christian Medical Fellowship, and a writer and editor. Her first book, *If Only*, is available now. She lives, works and worships in central London, blogs at jenniepollock.com and tweets as @missjenniep.

Can we benefit God?

PREPARE

Think of three things you are thankful for. These are gifts from the Lord that he didn't have to give you. Thank him for his lavish generosity.

READ

Job 22:1–30

EXPLORE

Can we benefit God (v 2)? Is there anything we can do or say that makes his existence better in any way?

On the one hand, of course, the answer is a resounding 'No!' – as Eliphaz's sarcastic question implies. God is infinite, all-powerful and completely satisfied in himself. There is nothing he needs, and nothing that we, the works of his hands, can give to him that he does not already own.

Nor can we take anything away from him. He is not diminished by anyone's rejection of his love. Nor is he depleted by our consumption of his gifts.

Yet this does not mean that he is indifferent to us. He loves us, and although we, like tiny, helpless infants, cannot add any benefit to him, still we can bring him great joy and pleasure. Just as loving parents are delighted when their children give them a crayon self-portrait, a wilted flower or even a toothless smile, so God is overjoyed with the gifts, however inadequate, we bring to him. The wonderful, mystifying, liberating truth is that our heavenly Father needs nothing from us, but exults in our tiniest acts of devotion and obedience.

'Can a man be of benefit to God? Can even a wise person benefit him?'

Job 22:2

RESPOND

Thank him for the marvellous gift of his love and the pleasure that his children bring to him. We come with empty hands, yet he is delighted that we come at all.

Bible in a year: Numbers 10,11; Acts 17

When God feels far away

PREPARE
Do you feel close to God or far from him today? Acknowledge where you are with him.

. . . .

READ
Job 23:1–17

EXPLORE
Have you ever felt the kind of desperation Job expresses in this chapter? We all have seasons when God feels far away, and our prayers seem like they are just hitting the ceiling.

What a contrast from Psalm 139, when the psalmist talks of the impossibility of escaping from God's presence and the futility of trying to hide from him. When we *don't* want him, he is everywhere; when we do, he is apparently nowhere to be found. And yet, in verse 10, Job reminds himself of the truth: 'But he knows the way that I take.' Even when we can't seem to find God, we are never out of sight to him.

God knew everything that was going on with Job. If you know the book, you'll know that at the end God shows up in all his glory and reveals that he has been listening to every word Job and his friends have said. The same is true for us.

Even when we can't see him or detect his presence, he is always with us, and his plan is to bring us forth as gold (v 10).

'But he knows the way that I take; when he has tested me, I shall come forth as gold.'
Job 23:10

RESPOND
It can be hard sitting, like Job, waiting in the silence, but one day our waiting will be over. Christ will return to live with us, and we will never have to search for him again (Revelation 21:2–4). Thank him for that coming day.

. . . .

Bible in a year: Numbers 12–14; Psalms 28,29

Saturday 5 March

Job 24:1–25

A day of justice

PREPARE

What issues in the news or in your community are on your heart today? Lay them before the Lord as you sit in his presence.

READ

Job 24:1–25

EXPLORE

In today's chapter, Job begins by looking at all the injustice around him – the dishonest prospering and appearing to get away with it; the poor driven deeper into despair. It seems as though God is turning a blind eye.

But then, in verse 18, Job remembers the bigger picture. The wicked may prosper for now, but this earth isn't all there is. A day will come when God will enact justice, and the wicked will be snatched away (v 19), forgotten, broken (v 20) and brought low (v 24).

This reminder can give us courage and resilience in the face of adversity, and it can help us to find at least some comfort in the 'why' questions of life. But also, Jesus commanded us to love our enemies. As believers, we shouldn't rejoice in all the bad things that are going to happen to bad people, but weep over their destruction and their hardness of heart, and should pray that they will come to repentance, not simply get their comeuppance. The truth is that in God's eyes, every sinner looks as bad as these people – we did, before Christ graciously saved us – and everyone is in need of his love and redemption.

'But God drags away the mighty by his power; though they become established, they have no assurance of life.'

Job 24:22

RESPOND

Pray for those you know who need salvation. Pray for your enemies, if you have any – not that they will be judged, but that they will be redeemed.

Bible in a year: Numbers 15,16; Acts 18

The river of delights

PREPARE

Are you hungry and thirsty for more of the Lord? Ask him to give you the hunger only he can satisfy.

. . . .

READ

Psalm 36

EXPLORE

This is a psalm about abundance. It begins by describing the extent of humanity's sinfulness. 'Even on their beds they plot evil' (v 4). Do they never stop for a minute?! But then in contrast, it describes the boundlessness of God's goodness. His love reaches to the heavens; his justice is as deep as the ocean (vs 5,6).

At the end of 2020, scientists exploring the bed of the Atlantic discovered a dozen previously unknown species of sea life. God had made these creatures on the fifth day of creation, knowing that we wouldn't find them until thousands of years later. Isn't that incredible? Vast as it is, though, creation is finite – it is possible for humans to see everything. But God, his attributes, his character and his gifts are infinite. We could swim in the depths of his justice for eternity and never find its limits.

More unfathomable still, this infinite, creative, holy God wants to share his goodness with us. One day we will join him in a feast, as Christ is at last united with his bride, the church (Revelation 19:6–9), but until then we can feast on his Word and his sustaining power, and drink from his 'river of delights' (v 8).

People ... feast in the abundance of your house; you give them drink from your river of delights.

Psalm 36:7,8

RESPOND

'Praise God from whom all blessings flow / Praise him all creatures here below / Praise him above ye heavenly host / Praise Father, Son and Holy Ghost'

*Thomas Ken, 1674.

. . . .

Bible in a year: Numbers 17–19; Acts 19

Job 25:1 – 26:14

Can we be right with God?

PREPARE

Prepare your heart by confessing your sins to God and receiving his forgiveness.

....

READ

Job 25:1 – 26:14

EXPLORE

In this short chapter, Bildad raises probably the most important question in the Bible: 'How then can a mortal be righteous before God?' (25:4). His timing wasn't great, asking it when Job was at his lowest ebb. And his attitude wasn't very helpful, either, since his purpose was to contradict Job's claims of his own righteousness. But still, it is a question we all need to confront – and to be able to answer for others.

Job probably lived before the Law had been given and before the system of priests and sacrifices had been established. Yet we know from chapter 1 that Job recognised the need to make regular sacrifices to atone for his sins. Job was diligent about these sacrifices, even making extra ones on behalf of his children, just in case they had sinned in their hearts (1:5).

The formalised system given when God made his covenant with Moses and the Israelites was incredibly burdensome, and almost impossible to keep up. In fact, the book of Hebrews tells us those sacrifices could never take away our sins (Hebrews 10:1–4). But there is hope. Christ, our perfect sacrifice, shed his blood 'once for all' to win 'eternal redemption' for those who believe in him (Hebrews 9:11–15).

> 'How then can a mortal be righteous before God?'
>
> **Job 25:4a**

RESPOND

Thank you, Lord Jesus, for dying for us, and making it possible for sinful mortals – including even me – to be made righteous before the Father.

....

Bible in a year: Numbers 20,21; Acts 20

A clear conscience

PREPARE

'Love the Lord your God with all your heart and with all your soul and with all your strength and with all your mind ... Love your neighbour as yourself' (Luke 10:27). How have you obeyed these commandments recently?

....

READ

Job 27:1–23

EXPLORE

How amazing that Job felt able to state, in today's key verse (v 6), that he *was* assured of his righteousness before God. As we saw in yesterday's reading, this was an almost impossible task, but Job – even after all his friends challenging him to examine his heart and life – was confident that his conscience was clear.

I don't think this was arrogance or self-deception; the whole premise of this book is that God himself declared that Job was 'blameless and upright, a man who fears God and shuns evil' (1:8).

As we saw yesterday, under the new covenant – the salvation bought for us by Jesus' blood – we are declared righteous once and for all. All our past, present and future sins have been washed away. And yet, we are still called to live holy lives (see 1 Peter 1:13–16), to be blameless and upright, to fear God and to shun evil. This is not to earn our salvation, but to reflect it – to be a witness to those around us, and to show the transforming power of God's Holy Spirit.

> 'I will maintain my innocence and never let go of it; my conscience will not reproach me as long as I live.'
> **Job 27:6**

RESPOND

Could you say confidently that you are blameless and upright? Ask God to help you see the areas where your life does not reflect the purity you have been given, and to continue to transform you from within.

....

Bible in a year: Numbers 22,23; Psalm 30

Buried treasure

PREPARE

What is your favourite feature of God's creation? Spend a moment thinking about it and praising God for it.

READ

Job 28:1–28

EXPLORE

In today's wonderfully poetic chapter, Job begins by celebrating what is known as 'human exceptionalism' – mankind's special, God-given abilities and mandate to explore and exploit the earth (vs 1–11). Only we, of all God's creatures, can dig mines, refine gold, and smelt iron. Only we are investigators, seeking to know and understand more about this planet we are living on and its universe. Thousands of years on from when this was written, we are still discovering new wonders on the earth, beneath the sea and above the skies. And thousands of years on, we still haven't managed to plumb the depths of wisdom.

You would think that as we grew in knowledge and understanding of the world, we would grow in wisdom at the same speed, but it often seems as though the very opposite is the case.

Job explains that this is because wisdom cannot be found in anything that is created, but only in the creator himself (vs 23–28). Fearing him – having an appropriate reverence for and honour of him – puts him in his rightful place and enables us to see clearly and understand rightly everything else under the sun.

> 'But where can wisdom be found? Where does understanding dwell?'
> **Job 28:12**

RESPOND

Wisdom is 'more precious than rubies' (Proverbs 8:11) but is freely and generously given to all who ask for it (James 1:5). Ask the Lord to give you these riches in increasing measure.

The good old days

PREPARE

Think back on a happy memory. Recall the joy of that moment or season. Thank God for his past blessings to you.

READ

Job 29:1–25

EXPLORE

'Oh, for the days when I was in my prime!' I suspect many of us can sympathise with Job's heart-cry in verse 4 of today's reading. Maybe we weren't all as highly respected or abundantly blessed as Job goes on to describe, but it is natural when we face difficulties or failing health to look back and long for happier, easier times. We may even have a nostalgia for past eras of history, when life was simpler (ignoring the fact that it was also usually more hazardous!).

How should we as believers think about the past? The Bible often commands God's people to recall their past. The Israelites were told to tell, year after year, the story of their rescue from Egypt and God's miraculous provision and protection. Jesus told us to break bread and drink wine in remembrance of him.

The purpose is not to make us nostalgic for 'the good old days', 'when the

Almighty was still with [us]' (29:5). Rather, the idea is that remembering what God did *then* will give us faith and hope for what he is doing *now*.

> 'Oh, for the days when I was in my prime, when God's intimate friendship blessed my house.'
>
> **Job 29:4**

RESPOND

'Father, thank you for giving us your Word that reveals your power and love at work in your people. Please help me to remember that you are still at work, just as you always have been. Help me to trust you for the future. Amen.'

Bible in a year: Numbers 26,27; Acts 22

Friday 11 March

Job 30:1–31

Help for the hurting

PREPARE
Settle your heart before the Lord. Ask him to speak to you today, and to give you a willing heart to hear and obey anything he says.

READ
Job 30:1–31

EXPLORE
What can we learn from a chapter like today's, in which Job is contrasting the different treatment he gets from people now that he is no longer prosperous and successful?

Perhaps we need to recognise ourselves in the people Job is accusing. How easily do we judge people by their outward success? How often do we praise and celebrate others while everything is going well, but turn our backs when they hit a rough patch? Sadly, this happens in churches at least as much as out in 'the world'. One friend recently told me that his church was incredibly supportive during his marriage preparation, but when his marriage was in trouble, there was little help to be found.

It can be hard for those who are hurting to hear from God or feel his comfort – as was the case for Job. They need us more than ever to press in and demonstrate God's unending, unfailing love.

We may not know what to say or do, but letting them know we care and are standing with them in prayer is a good place to start.

> 'Yet when I hoped for good, evil came; when I looked for light, then came darkness.'
>
> **Job 30:26**

RESPOND
Do you know someone who is struggling just now? Maybe they haven't been at church for a while or have seemed down when you talk to them. Pray for them, asking God to guide you as you reach out and share his compassion.

Bible in a year: Numbers 28,29; Psalm 31

Rewarding righteousness?

PREPARE

Pay attention to your breathing for a few breaths. Thank God for the gift of air and the miracle of our bodies absorbing what is good and expelling what is harmful.

READ

Job 31:1–40

EXPLORE

'But I've done everything right!' This was the heart-cry of someone I was praying for once. She wouldn't say she was as blameless as Job, but she had always sought to follow God's Word and his leading in her life. Yet in one particular area she felt as though God had let her down, as though he hadn't kept his side of the bargain.

It is easy to slip into the sense that life isn't fair, especially when things are going badly. We can subconsciously believe that God has a duty to reciprocate when we obey and serve him.

In reality, he has already done so much for us – he created this world for us to live in, and gives us not only our daily bread but our daily breath! The very air we breathe is a precious gift from him, without which we would be nothing. And that is before we even mention him sending his precious Son to be sacrificed on our behalf and give us his eternal life. Who are we to ask anything more of such a Father?

> 'Let God weigh me in honest scales and he will know that I am blameless.'
>
> **Job 31:6**

RESPOND

Our worship and obedience are not bargaining tools to gain more blessings, but appropriate and necessary responses to the life, love and salvation we have already received. Thank the Lord for his abundant gifts – and repent of the times you have felt entitled.

Bible in a year: Numbers 30,31; Acts 23

Hope in the Lord

PREPARE

What are you hoping for? Or are you despairing that things will ever get better? Acknowledge to God what you are feeling today.

READ

Psalm 37

EXPLORE

This psalm could be a response to yesterday's chapter of Job, couldn't it? The psalmist reiterates over and over again the truth that God sees the deeds of both the wicked and the righteous, and they will be treated fairly in the final reckoning.

Verses 23 and 24 seem to speak right into Job's situation: 'The LORD makes firm the steps of the one who delights in him; though he may stumble, he will not fall, for the LORD upholds him with his hand.' Job has definitely been stumbling through much of what we have read this week. He has been beset with doubt, concerned that God's justice seems far off and that he has been abandoned. But the wonderful truth is that 'the Lord upholds him with his hand'.

Trust in the Lord. Hope in him. Delight in him. Pursue righteousness. Do not fret. These are the words the psalmist would speak to Job, and that he speaks to us today. When it seems as though all is lost, choose to believe the truth that God has a good purpose, and he will not let you go.

> Hope in the LORD and keep his way. He will exalt you to inherit the land; when the wicked are destroyed, you will see it.
>
> **Psalm 37:34**

RESPOND

'Father God, thank you that you will enact justice in its time. Thank you that because of my faith in your Son's sacrifice, I am counted righteous and can be assured of my security in you. Help me always to hope in you. Amen.'

Bible in a year: Numbers 32,33; Acts 24

" I DON'T GO TO CHURCH BUT I DO BELIEVE IN GOD "

95% of under-18s don't go to church BUT many are open to exploring faith.

Together, we can reach the 95!
Find out more at **the95.org.uk**

Scripture Union

The wisdom books

Three books in the Bible are usually regarded as 'wisdom' literature: Job, Proverbs and Ecclesiastes. Sometimes the Song of Songs and certain Psalms are seen in this category and Catholic and Orthodox churches include the Wisdom of Solomon and Sirach (Ecclesiasticus) as well. This genre is not exclusive to the Bible, it was common in many ancient cultures.

Wisdom literature focuses on advice for everyday life. There is little emphasis on the bigger themes of the Scriptures. So things such as the Temple, the exodus and the detailed Old Testament laws for example, which figure large in the rest of the Bible, hardly get a mention. Wisdom books are focused on human life concerns rather than history. They address individuals rather than the nation.

What is wisdom?
Dictionary definitions include ideas such as good judgement, using your knowledge and experience, even plain common sense. The Bible, however, roots wisdom not in ourselves but in our attitude to God: 'The fear of the LORD is the beginning of wisdom' (Proverbs 9:10). According to the book of James, it's a freely given gift from God (James 1:5). One helpful definition in this context is this: 'Wisdom is the ability to make godly choices in life.'* This makes the *biblical* wisdom literature distinct from other kinds.

The three wisdom books in the Bible, not surprisingly, have different characteristics. Proverbs – obviously! – is made up of proverbs: pithy, wise sayings. These give us practical rules for living the good life. The other two books, on the other hand, are longer reflections on the meaning of life in the form of monologue (Ecclesiastes) and dialogue (Job). Each of the books is interesting in its own way but how do we make sense of them, particularly in our regular Bible reading? Here are three practical suggestions.

1 Read the *whole* of each book
As with every part of the Bible, it's important to see the whole picture. Try to take time to read each book as a whole rather than as small

sections. This doesn't take as long as you might imagine, especially when compared with time spent watching TV or films! Job and Proverbs can each be read in less than two hours and Ecclesiastes in only 30 minutes. Some people enjoy binge watching TV, so why not do some binge Bible reading?!

2 Try to understand what the whole book is about

Getting an overview is not always easy, especially with Proverbs where the structure is very loose. Even here though, there is a simple structure. It's sometimes divided into three sections: chapters 1–9, 10–24 and 25–31. In the case of Job, only in the final few chapters (38ff) do we get God's perspective on things. And in Ecclesiastes, you might say that the explanation comes only in the last two verses (12:13,14)! But without this perspective, we may well misunderstand the overall argument and wrongly pluck out individual verses. Is it *really* true that wicked people always live in terror (Job 18:11)?

3 Be careful when focusing on individual verses

It's all too easy to pluck out one idea from a book and give it a wrong emphasis or meaning. A friend once teased me with these words from Proverbs because I'd overslept: 'A

little sleep, a little slumber, a little folding of the hands to rest – and poverty will come on you like a thief and scarcity like an armed man' (Proverbs 6:10,11). I'm grateful that a little sleep doesn't lead to poverty! Just because certain *words* are in Scripture doesn't make them true. God chastised Job's friends for saying things to Job that weren't true (Job 42:7,8).

The wisdom books are a great gift from the past but much more importantly, from God. Through them, he wants to teach us important lessons about the meaning of life!

Writer **Emlyn Williams**

Useful resources

*Gordon D. Fee and Douglas Stuart, *How to Read the Bible for All Its Worth,* fourth edition, Zondervan, 2014.

The Bible Project Wisdom series: https://tinyurl.com/n3w8dwf6

The winner takes it all

About the writer
John Gay

John Gay is a Cornishman, married with two children. Following in Jesus' footsteps, he trained as a carpenter and is now a shepherd as a Team Vicar in the Brixham Mission Community.

'In the land of Uz there lived a man whose name was Job. This man was blameless and upright; he feared God and shunned evil' (1:1). The Book of Job is often portrayed as a study of suffering. That is only half the story. Its roots are deeply embedded in chapters 1 and 2. Look back now to remind yourself of its beginnings. What is going on? Who are the principal characters? What is their relationship? Who pulls the strings? Who's in charge? Who allows what and why?

By the end of chapter 2, we see the scenario. In a spiritual battle, God wagers the accusing Satan that Job will not curse God even once, no matter what misfortune befalls him. Suddenly, the kingdom of heaven, God's almighty sovereignty, everything is at stake, on the faith of one man, a god-fearing stranger!

Job knows nothing of this – why his life changes so radically, losing status, family, friends and health; nor, that on his shoulders rests *everything*. Thus, one careless curse against God could deliver all into the hands of the Evil One (1:8–11; 2:5–10).

His three 'comforting friends' are no comfort. Eliphaz says Job must have deserved his misfortune by sinning; Bildad criticises Job's insistence on his righteousness and Zophar reminds Job that God not only punishes the wicked, but that Job is getting off lightly! Job remains defiant; he has done no wrong by God, but rails 'where is God' and why is this happening to him? Time for the young Elihu to join in...

Do you hear what I hear?

PREPARE:

'For now we see only a reflection as in a mirror; then we shall see face to face. Now I know in part; then I shall know fully, even as I am fully known' (1 Corinthians 13:12).

READ
Job 32:1–22

EXPLORE

Job has so far only spoken directly with his three so-called friends. It has not gone well (see *Way In*). Job also talks to God but neither hears nor sees anything from him.

Chapter 32 suddenly introduces a new character, Elihu, a young man featuring neither before or after these next 6 chapters (Job 32–37). Many commentators consider him a later addition, an irrelevance – or, some kind of foreshadowing of Christ (see for example, 33:23–26), setting out Job's faults while giving him good advice. Neither Job nor God speaks with him.

Elihu states: 'It is not only the old who are wise, not only the aged who understand what is right. Therefore I say: listen to me; I too will tell you what I know' (vs 9,10). Is Elihu acting as a sort of bridge between Job's human complaints and God's inalienable holiness and sovereign power?

Like anyone, Elihu is capable of seeing the things of God (even if only dimly) and of man. And sometimes the young shake us out of our complacency, as has, for example, ecologist campaigner Greta Thunberg. Will we listen though when the young (or anyone else) talk sense?

> 'But it is the spirit in a person, the breath of the Almighty, that gives them understanding.'
> **Job 32:8**

RESPOND

We may only see and sense God partially at present (eg 1 Corinthians 13:12). Who is our 'bridge' to help us see God more clearly?

Sympathy for the devil

PREPARE
'But Jesus immediately said to them: 'Take courage! It is I. Don't be afraid' (Matthew 14:27).

READ
Job 33:1–33

EXPLORE
Elihu takes Job to task in verses 8–12. It is true, in his discourse with his friends, Job unfailingly protested his innocence of any sin and became angry that God was neither taking notice, nor giving him justice. Remember, all this is taking place in the context of a wager. God has promised to do nothing to intervene during the appointed time. God is not powerless, but simply keeping his word to Satan (2:6)!

Surprising though this may be, the wager is not about enmity, but breaking the first and third commandments – rejecting God's love by cursing him. God can deal with sin, but is unwilling to force Satan, Job or us to go against our will, even if we end up abandoning God. Fortunately, although Job may have faults, cursing the Lord and rejecting him are not among them!

Elihu therefore makes an excellent point to forgiven sinners: 'And they will go to others and say, "I have sinned, and I have perverted what is right, but I did not get what I deserved. God has delivered me from going down to the pit, and I shall live to enjoy the light of life"' (vs 27,28).

> 'Then that person can pray to God and find favour with him, they will see God's face and shout for joy; he will restore them to full well-being.'
>
> **Job 33:26**

RESPOND
Elihu reminded Job about the possibility of God's forgiveness. Is that a message you need to hear today? Read 1 John 1:9.

Bible in a year: Numbers 36; Deuteronomy 1; Psalm 32

If I could turn back time

PREPARE

'Repent and be baptised, every one of you, in the name of Jesus Christ for the forgiveness of your sins. And you will receive the gift of the Holy Spirit' (Acts 2:38).

READ

Job 34:1–37

EXPLORE

Elihu demonstrates himself to be guilty of misunderstanding through lack of knowledge. He understands no more than Job or the friends about the background situation. Yet, in verse 33, he asks an important question: should we expect God to forgive us if we do not repent?

When we do something wrong, guilt can lead us to try to avoid discovery. Our default position is to close down the possibilities of being found out. Should our misdemeanour be exposed, we then often try to deny our guilt, at least to begin with. It is human nature.

The Scriptures teach us that we all sin (Romans 3:23). No one is exempt. But we also learn that this does not have to define our lives. Things can be turned around if we are prepared to humble ourselves before God and ask his forgiveness; ultimately, he is the only one who can do this for us. Jesus teaches us that repentance brings huge rewards to those who are willing to take that step (eg Luke 15:7).

> '"Teach me what I cannot see; if I have done wrong, I will not do so again." Should then God reward you on your terms?'
>
> **Job 34:32,33**

RESPOND

How do we deal with our own sense of guilt? How do we handle the guilt of others? Can we find it in ourselves to forgive as our heavenly Father forgives us? The Lord's Prayer is more challenging than we think!

Bible in a year: Deuteronomy 2,3; Acts 26

Thursday 17 March
Job 35:1–16

Reach out, I'll be there

PREPARE
'Trust in the Lᴏʀᴅ with all your heart and lean not on your own understanding; in all your ways submit to him, and he will make your paths straight' (Proverbs 3:5,6).

....

READ
Job 35:1–16

EXPLORE
Earlier, Job had complained that God was indifferent and distant to his condition (Job 23). Elihu refutes this idea: 'No one says, "Where is God my Maker?"' (v 10). Really? Is Job alone in thinking that God is not on their case? Can't we sometimes feel that God isn't listening or is absent when we do not sense his presence or intervention in our lives?

Job had protested that he has 'closely followed his [God's] steps' and 'treasured the words of his mouth' (23:11,12). Was God ignoring or forgetting about him? Was Job right to complain his case was not being heard? Does Elihu have a point? Do we think that when God is not serving our perceived needs, he is not interested in us? Does an apparent lack of answer to prayer suggest we cannot trust God? Do we (unintentionally) merely reduce God to being our skivvy?

Jesus said: 'Surely I am with you always, to the very end of the age' (Matthew 28:20). Will it not be so? In times of crisis, we can think the worst. It is then we are called to dig deep in faith and pray to God through the Holy Spirit to help us.

> 'People cry out under a load of oppression; they plead for relief from the arm of the powerful. But no one says, "Where is God my Maker?"'
> **Job 35:9,10**

RESPOND
The old hymn 'Trust and Obey' is a great encouragement to hold on to our faith through trust in the Lord.* What other resources might help us?

*John Henry Sammis (1846–1919).

....

Bible in a year: Deuteronomy 4,5; Acts 27

God knows I'm good

PREPARE

'He causes his sun to rise on the evil and the good, and sends rain on the righteous and the unrighteous' (Matthew 5:45).

....

READ

Job 36:1–33

EXPLORE

Why does God allow bad things to happen to good people? Why do the wicked seem to prosper? Job thinks he is hard done by, while the greedy and morally doubtful seem to live off the fat of the land!

Jesus said that the sun and rain settle on the good and the bad equally (Matthew 5:45); Elihu reminds us God is right and just in all he does and permits. Thus, when the time comes, God's justice will fall on all. Previous deeds may be taken into account but ultimately faith or lack of it will determine where eternal life is spent (vs 5–11).

Elihu's words here tend to echo Bildad's criticism that Job is too self-righteous (Job 8:1–3). Is the penny dropping for Job? After all, which of us is truly good? Have we never broken the speed limit, for example?! If there is sin, it will be found out and an account of it must be given.

Elihu continues: 'one who has perfect knowledge is with you' (v 4). Whether or not this refers to God or Elihu, God knows Job's predicament and has faith in him. Job's own faith in God, or lack of it, will determine his outcome (2:10b).

'I get my knowledge from afar; I will ascribe justice to my Maker. Be assured that my words are not false; one who has perfect knowledge is with you.'
Job 36:3,4

RESPOND

God knows we are not perfect as he is, but the Holy Spirit can train us toward holiness. What is God working on in your life? How can you cooperate with that today?

....

Bible in a year: Deuteronomy 6,7; Psalm 33

Bitter-sweet symphony

PREPARE

'Whoever speaks on their own does so to gain personal glory, but he who seeks the glory of the one who sent him is a man of truth; there is nothing false about him' (John 7:18).

READ

Job 37:1-24

EXPLORE

In this, Elihu's last discourse, God's mighty power and sovereignty over all things is the subject and the prelude to God himself speaking (chapter 38). At chapter end, Elihu stops as suddenly as he started, but not before highlighting the undeniable fact of Job's miserable experience and God's response to it: God is still in charge (vs 23,24).

Job's complaint all along has been: where is God? Has he gone AWOL? Why hasn't he helped? Doesn't he care? Elihu answers these complaints in God's absence. In a way, he almost does so to prepare Job for what is to come. But Job is listening to a man. What could Elihu say that Job could not have gleaned by his own wisdom?

How do we hear God speaking to us alongside his word in Scripture? Can we hear it in the voice of another telling us about the things of God? Do we notice the Holy Spirit's blessings in our everyday experience? Do we see it in creation? Do we sense it in prayer? How does God's awesome majesty make itself plain, so that we become 'wise in heart' (v 24)?

'God comes in awesome majesty. The Almighty is beyond our reach and exalted in power; in his justice and great righteousness, he does not oppress.'

Job 37:22,23

RESPOND

How might God be speaking to you today? In 1 Thessalonians 5:16–24 Paul encourages us in our prayerful relationship with God. Allow the Holy Spirit to help you now.

Bible in a year: Deuteronomy 8,9; Acts 28

Don't leave me this way

PREPARE

'But the fruit of the Spirit is love, joy, peace, forbearance, kindness, goodness, faithfulness, gentleness and self-control. Against such things there is no law' (Galatians 5:22,23).

READ

Psalm 38

EXPLORE

Job could have written this psalm. It sums up his situation. Everything is wrong; he feels that God is punishing him; his critics are unsympathetic; he feels feeble and crushed and God seems absent (v 4).

We might sometimes think God leaves us periodically to our own strength. Our prayer life may not be so strong, or maybe we have been taking God for granted. The apparent absence of God's blessings and presence may discourage us, but should we hold it against him? Could we see such trials as a blessing that builds spiritual resilience?

Jesus himself was not immune to this: he spent much time in prayer on his own, while frustrated at others' lack of faith (eg Luke 6:12; Mark 9:17–29). Even *he* wondered why after three years of ministry his Father had apparently abandoned him on the cross (Matthew 27:46).

The important word is 'apparently'. It might seem like God was/is not there, but he always is and will always pick up his faithful ones and stand them on their feet before him. Prayerful communication and trust between him and us are the key.

LORD, do not forsake me; do not be far from me, my God. Come quickly to help me, my LORD and my Saviour.

Psalm 38:21,22

RESPOND

Take time to consider God's place in your heart and your place in his. Where do you stand today? Jesus' prayer time was a gateway into the precious company of his heavenly Father. It can also be yours.

Bible in a year: Deuteronomy 10,11; Romans 1

Monday 21 March
Job 38:1–21

The boxer

PREPARE
'Send me your light and your faithful care, let them lead me; let them bring me to your holy mountain, to the place where you dwell' (Psalm 43:3).

READ
Job 38:1–21

EXPLORE
BOOM! The Lord speaks! Now follow four chapters where Job is challenged and rocked to the core by the voice of God. In these chapters, God asks Job a barrage of questions. Some are in clusters like a boxer using his jab to soften up an opponent. And all have the underlying question: 'Who are you to challenge me, who made everything, and by whom does everything that lives, live?'

Job now needs to decide. Is God right? Did he create the world as he says? Is he in charge? Or is there another? If not God, then who is in control of the world and Job's own destiny? Job could be tempted to think this 'deity' speaking to him is a little too shouty! Why has God left him in painful destitution?

One senses that Satan may be trying to play his last cards from the shadows by suggesting to Job: 'If there is unrest in your world how can your God be in charge? Surely a wise and righteous person like you can be master of your own destiny! Why is God shouting at you? Call his bluff!'

> Then the LORD spoke to Job out of the storm. He said: 'Who is this that obscures my plans with words without knowledge?'
> **Job 38:1,2**

RESPOND
The Lord speaks! Now Job is quiet. God has had to shout to get Job's attention. Is that how it is with us? Could God speak to us quietly in his unique way and still have us listen?

Bible in a year: Deuteronomy 12–14; Romans 2

Who are you?

PREPARE

'I am the Alpha and the Omega,' says the Lord God, 'who is, and who was, and who is to come, the Almighty' (Revelation 1:8)

. . . .

READ

Job 38:22–41

EXPLORE

God challenges Job further, using the natural world to demonstrate that Job is a very small fish in a big pond. What was Job thinking now? Did Job take in that of all the people to whom God could have spoken, it was him? OK, he was being put in his place, but this was God Almighty speaking, and to him directly!

Job is receiving individual attention now in a way he never did before his misfortune. God is answering his prayer. Job demands justice from God on account of his faith. He finds that when asked on what basis he can claim rights, he has none. Who has done what the Lord has done? Can Job even look him in the eye?

He is confronted with the works of the Lord. Has he considered this before? Even if Job had built a house and overseen a city and its people, compared to the greatness of all that God has done, Job is definitely small fry. The Lord's works testify to his glory. What has Job to offer in return?

'Do you know the laws of the heavens? Can you set up God's dominion over the earth?'
Job 38:33

RESPOND

'Praise to the Lord! Oh, let all that is in me adore him! / All that hath life and breath, come now with praises before him! / Let the Amen, Sound from his people again; Gladly for aye we adore him'

*Joachim Neander 1650–1680.

. . . .

Bible in a year: Deuteronomy 15,16; Psalm 34

Stand by your man

PREPARE

'The LORD is my rock, my fortress and my deliverer; my God is my rock, in whom I take refuge, my shield and the horn of my salvation, my stronghold' (Psalm 18:2).

READ

Job 39:1–30

EXPLORE

God turns his onslaught to examples from the animal kingdom. Do you? Can you? Who has? Will it? Does it? His questions to Job are relentless and one imagines Job staggering around trying to regain his senses and perspective.

Why does God push Job so much? Could it be that he feels he still has a point to make; not to Job, but to Satan who has been conspicuous by his absence since chapter 2? Satan, the accuser, the pretender to the throne of heaven, would be looking to lay down the excuse that God has been overly lenient with Job and therefore the wager was not fairly conducted. By grilling Job in this way, no one can lay that charge at God's door.

The downside is that Job is under attack from every side and, in weakness, might curse God for what has befallen him. The upside is God's confidence in his man – God knows of what Job is made and who is his stronghold. God has faith in his man. Will his man return that faith?

'Does the eagle soar at your command and build its nest on high? It dwells on a cliff and stays there at night; a rocky crag is its stronghold.'

Job 39:27,28

RESPOND

We can place our trust in worldly things until they become the 'rocks' on which we build our lives (Psalm 71:3). Do you take enough 'time out' to be with our rock of refuge? What could you change?

Bible in a year: Deuteronomy 17,18; Romans 3

Stop! In the name of love

PREPARE

'The arrogance of man will be brought low and human pride humbled; the LORD alone will be exalted in that day' (Isaiah 2:17).

READ

Job 40:1–24

EXPLORE

Job has been tested physically and mentally by Satan since chapter 1. He has been berated by his friends for having sinned (Eliphaz), being self-righteous (Bildad) and deserving worse for his sin (Zophar). The independently minded Elihu has alluded to somewhat the same even though his criticism is more constructive. God has already reproved Job for his presumption to self-righteousness (38:2).

Job settles for a bit of a climb down. Faced with a barrage of questions from God that he cannot answer, what could he say (vs 4,5)? Not enough, evidently! 'I will say no more' doesn't cut it!

The Lord presses on, drilling down to test Job spiritually again. In verses 7–14 and then through to the end of chapter 41, full acknowledgement is sought from Job of the Lord's majesty, glory, justice and sovereignty over all things. Dare Job contend that he can stand before the justice of God and win? Others may be listening too: Elihu, the three friends, the reader of this book… and, of course, Satan.

Job is at breaking point – will it all be too much? How would we fare in that situation?

> Then Job answered the LORD: 'I am unworthy – how can I reply to you? I put my hand over my mouth. I spoke once, but I have no answer – twice, but I will say no more.'

Job 40:3–5

RESPOND

As with Job here, pride can easily trip us up. Humility is costly, even if we can get over our pride. When we're facing God, pride will never win! Pray for humility to be your default position.

Bible in a year: Deuteronomy 19,20; Romans 4

Stand and deliver

PREPARE
'For he has been mindful of the humble state of his servant. From now on all generations will call me blessed, for the Mighty One has done great things for me – holy is his name' (Luke 1:48,49).

READ
Job 41:1–34

EXPLORE

God continues to test Job spiritually. It could appear that he wants to see Job crack under the strain and utter that curse that would see God lose his wager (Job 1:8–12). The Lord tries a new twist. He compares Job to himself and asks him: 'Could you control the Leviathan, the mightiest of sea creatures? Are you the Almighty?'

If Job says he can go where God goes, do the mighty works God does, is able to control all things in heaven and earth as God is able, then Job puts himself in the place of God and curses God as inferior! Even if Job was to *think* he could do these things, God knows he can't! But will Job, out of his suffering and wretchedness, lose patience and say, 'Yes, I can!'?

That would be enough for Satan. No doubt he can hardly believe his luck!

This trick would normally be his own last throw of the dice, and there is God doing it for him. Surely Job's misery will make him crack and win the prize for Satan.

> 'Who then is able to stand against me? Who has a claim against me that I must pay?'
> **Job 41:10,11**

RESPOND
Sometimes, like Job, we find ourselves under great stress: everything seems to be working against us. Do we react prayerfully, or with frustration, even rage? In times of testing, who do we turn to and how?

Bible in a year: Deuteronomy 21,22; Psalm 35

Ray of light

PREPARE

'And we know that in all things God works for the good of those who love him, who have been called according to his purpose' (Romans 8:28).

READ
Job 42:1–16

EXPLORE

God's majesty drives Job to repentance and humility (vs 5,6). Satan's wager is lost; the kingdom will not be his. One frail man who will not curse his creator wins the day for the Lord. Satan's only way back is to do what Job did; repent utterly. Instead, Satan will try again, this time against Jesus. The stakes will include God's own self, and death, Satan's last stronghold. But Satan will again be defeated – utterly (1 Corinthians 15:57).

Job's story is also God's story. It was never so at the beginning, but since the Fall (Genesis 3) suffering has been an abnormality in our world. But still 'the light shines in the darkness, and the darkness has not overcome it' (John 1:5). God is merciful to those who repent and are put right with him (see vs 7–9). Job's fortunes are restored to him and indeed doubled in measure for family, wealth and lifespan (vs 12–15).

What is revealed here is the sovereign might, majesty and glory of God seen in the just, generous and steadfast love of the Lord toward those who love him. Such is the reward for saints.

> The LORD blessed the latter part of Job's life more than the former part.
>
> **Job 42:12**

RESPOND

'He has shown you, O mortal, what is good. And what does the LORD require of you? To act justly and to love mercy and to walk humbly with your God' (Micah 6:8). Now all we need is to do it.

Bible in a year: Deuteronomy 23,24; Romans 5

Sunday 27 March
Psalm 39:1–13

Homeward bound

PREPARE

'The death he [Jesus] died, he died to sin once for all; but the life he lives, he lives to God' (Romans 6:10).

READ

Psalm 39:1–13

EXPLORE

The psalms often speak to the human condition, in this case to death. How long have I got and will the Lord be merciful?

Other than wishing to put their affairs in order, why the author of this psalm should want to know how long they have left to live we do not know (v 4). Yet perhaps if we knew the time and manner of our passing away, we would probably spend our time trying to avoid death rather than living life in its fullness.

Our mortal life may be short, but is given to us to love, recognise and praise our Creator. Then we give thanks and realise that through Jesus, our lives can be brought to eternal life and holiness.

When God created us, he didn't create automatons, but people with free will to love him or not as they desire. Those who love him are being sanctified (being made perfect), and will continue to love him in the next life. Those who reject him will separate themselves from him for ever. Length of life or the manner of our death matters less than where we are going, because wherever that is, it will be for eternity.

Show me, Lord, my life's end and the number of my days ... the span of my years is as nothing before you. Everyone is but a breath...

Psalm 39:4,5

RESPOND

'Thank you for all the days you have given me. Help me to live today and every day in the light of your word. Amen.'

Bible in a year: Deuteronomy 25,26; Romans 6

Jesus is Alive!

This Easter experience the amazing story of God's plan to save his people. Guardians of Ancora, developed by Scripture Union, is a free-to-download game that brings the stories of the Bible to life.

Experience the joy of knowing Jesus is alive and celebrate God's gift to all. Bring the story of the resurrection to life in the heart of a child this Easter. Download Guardians of Ancora for free and live the incredible adventures of Easter.

Download and play
Guardians of Ancora FOR FREE

 GUARDIANS OF **ANCORA**   Find out more at guardiansofancora.com   Scripture Union

Matthew 24,25

Waiting for his coming

Over the next week, we will be looking at two chapters from Matthew's Gospel known as the 'Olivet Discourse', in which Jesus prophesies about the destruction of Jerusalem and the end of this age. We will be shocked by great suffering and challenged to be on the alert. These chapters have been interpreted in numerous ways, and many have tried to answer the disciples' question in Matthew 24:3: 'When will this happen, and what will be the sign?'

As the events of the COVID-19 pandemic unfolded around the world, a lot of apocalyptic language was used in an attempt to explain what was going on. Some suggested that the end was near, others that it was judgement for sin. For many of us, we could suddenly relate to the people in Noah's days, eating and drinking and getting married (24:38) until disaster struck. With these events fresh in our memories, this is a good time to look at what Jesus actually said. Perhaps living through a global pandemic has given us a new perspective on the instability of this life and on the hope that we have as Christians for a future that is certain.

Whether we live through pandemics, natural disasters, war or personal tragedy, our question should not be the extent to which current events relate to prophecies in Matthew, Daniel or Revelation, but simply whether we are ready today if Jesus either returns or calls us home. When he comes, will he find us doing what he has asked us to do (24:46)?

About the writer
Alison Allen

After 14 years involved in mission in and from Romania, Alison returned to the UK in 2014 and now lives in Suffolk with her husband, two young children and three cats. Alison is currently working in the local Public Health department, whilst researching millennials in international mission for a PhD.

Endure to the end

PREPARE

Take a few moments to pray about one of the major news stories happening right now. Pray for Christian brothers and sisters living through it.

READ

Matthew 24:1–14

EXPLORE

I don't think Jesus' answer to the disciples' question (v 4) was quite what they were looking for. They probably wanted a nice, tidy checklist, with times, dates and key events. Something they could plan their lives around. Many people are still looking for – and indeed trying to create – this kind of list. They take obscure verses from this section of Matthew, from Daniel's prophecy (Daniel 9–12) and from Revelation, and try to tie them to world events in order to predict when and how Christ will return.

The point of Jesus' response seems to be that 'yes, bad stuff will happen': there will be both natural and man-made disasters (v 7). Christians will be persecuted to the point of death (v 9) and many will give up their faith (vs 10,12). We certainly see this happening today.

So how does Jesus want us to respond?

We find two things in this passage. In verse 13, we are told to 'stand firm' or 'endure'. Endurance isn't fun or pleasant; it's about keeping going when things are tough. Jesus never promised life would be easy. He did promise hope for a better life to come. Secondly, Jesus invites us to play a part in sharing his gospel message with those who haven't heard (v 14).

> '…but the one who stands firm to the end will be saved.'
>
> **Matthew 24:13**

RESPOND

Pray for anyone you know who is struggling to 'stand firm' in faith in the face of their present trials.

Bible in a year: Deuteronomy 27,28; Romans 7

Ready, set, run!

PREPARE

Think of some of the biblical names for Jesus: Emmanuel, Shepherd, Redeemer, Light, Friend etc. Thank him that he is all of these to you.

READ

Matthew 24:15–35

EXPLORE

This is one of those passages of Scripture that we Christians tend either to have strong opinions about – or completely ignore because we don't understand it. The reference to Daniel in verse 15 can be found in Daniel 9:27, 11:31 and 12:11. Daniel's prophecy is clearly about the desecration of the Temple in Jerusalem which took place in 168 BC. This then leads to the interpretation that Jesus is predicting the destruction of the Temple in Jerusalem that took place in AD 70, when Christians did indeed flee to the hills (v 16). However, others argue that this passage – and those in Daniel – refer to the end of this age, when Christ will return.

Whatever your stance (or if you haven't thought about it), Jesus is teaching us here to be aware of what is going on around us (vs 32,33) and to be ready to move in whatever way is necessary (vs 16–20).

If there's one thing the Coronavirus pandemic taught us, it's to hold our plans and our normality lightly. Things may change at any moment. You won't always have time to go back for your cloak (vs 17,18). In a world that is constantly changing, the only thing we can truly depend on are the words of Jesus (v 35).

'Heaven and earth will pass away, but my words will never pass away.'

Matthew 24:35

RESPOND

Meditate on the words of Matthew 28:20b: 'And surely I am with you always, to the very end of the age!'

Bible in a year: Deuteronomy 29,30; Psalm 36

Today's the day

PREPARE
Still your heart before the Lord and ask him to speak to you today.

· ·

READ
Matthew 24:36–51

EXPLORE
Jesus uses different images in this passage to reinforce the sense of verses 36, 42 and 44: nobody knows when he will return. First, his return is compared to the time of Noah (vs 37–39), when people were carrying on as normal until the moment the flood arrived. Secondly, we imagine two people working together (vs 40,41), one of whom is taken. Thirdly, Jesus asks, wouldn't we take precautions to prevent house-breaking (v 43)? And lastly, we are to compare the examples of a faithful and an evil servant, each left in charge when the master is away.

So, let's ponder the question in verse 45. Are we being faithful in the things he has given us to do? Are we using our position to bless others or to take advantage of them (compare verse 45 with verse 49)? I find it easy to imagine positive changes in my life that will start tomorrow. But when tomorrow comes, well, often my good intentions get pushed back by another week or two! Jesus' point is that it is *now* that matters: we cannot know when he will return, so we need to live as if it might be today.

> 'Who then is the faithful and wise servant, whom the master has put in charge of the servants in his household to give them their food at the proper time?'
> **Matthew 24:45**

RESPOND
Are there aspects of your life that you don't think Jesus would like if he returned right now? Talk to him about things you know need to change. Talk with a Christian friend or leader who could walk with you through the change.

· ·

Bible in a year: Deuteronomy 31,32; Romans 8

Extra or enough?

PREPARE
Pray for a friend or family member who doesn't know Jesus.

. . . .

READ
Matthew 25:1–13

EXPLORE
Jesus tells this parable to underscore the point made in yesterday's passage: we must be ready at any moment because we do not know when he will return.

The virgins in this passage had a role similar to that of modern-day bridesmaids: to prepare and accompany the bride on her wedding day. It is an honour to have this role, and there is excitement and anticipation. The UK tradition is for the bride to be late; but in this case it is the bridegroom they are waiting for. In fact, he's so late they all fall asleep.

We are told that the difference between the wise and foolish virgins is whether or not they had brought *extra* oil for their lamps. I guess the foolish virgins assumed either that what they had would be enough, or that they could nip out and buy more tomorrow. It was an assumption that cost them their place at the feast. Having enough but no more wasn't enough in the long run.

The implication is that to be wise is to recognise that Jesus might come at any time and be prepared for that possibility. Following Jesus doesn't mean simply sitting back, complacently awaiting his return. We need to be fully committed in our living for him, not just going through the motions. When Jesus comes, we won't be able to rely on someone else's extra oil.

'The wise ones, however, took oil in jars along with their lamps.'
Matthew 25:4

RESPOND
How prepared do you feel? Talk to Jesus about it.

. . . .

Bible in a year: Deuteronomy 33,34; Romans 9